The Fatl

"Give this book to the fathers you knov [barcode] and-
ing the archetypal ground of fatherhood ... all, especially
if we are trying to be a father and a husba ... well as a wife's lover and best
friend while trying to know our sons and daughters. Here the Original Images
of fatherhood help transform the false conventional world into creativity and
the true challenge of fatherhood developing a passion for life."

—Dirk Evers, Ph.D., Training Analyst,
C.G. Jung Institute, Zurich

"This work addresses one of the most important personal and societal issues
of our time: fathering. Harris, a Jungian analyst, draws on the rituals of primary
groups, Greek myths, and religious sources to investigate what was involved
in fathering in the past and what is required in our time. This is not a "how to"
or "cookbook" of formulas or steps for being a father; rather, Harris develops
a multifaceted view of fathering that is an individual process that challenges
each person's uniqueness, courage, and resolve. I have no doubt that if we
attempted to live the process he sets before us in this book, it would transform
the world for the better."

—Dr. J. Linn Mackey, Professor of Interdisciplinary Studies,
Appalachian State University

"A life-changing book! Bud Harris leads us into the deep and yearned for spirit
of fatherhood that inspires us to live life with conscious passion. He skillfully
weaves a tapestry of mythical images that guide our search for the personal
father who offers form to our lives and the grandfather who opens our heart
to mystery. Behind them stand the archetypal patterns of fathering that place
us in meaningful connection to the larger story. And even beyond that, Harris
brings us to profound reconciliation with the transcendent father who calls us
into the mists of our unseeable future and breathes spirit into the heart of our
existence."

—Les Rhodes, M.A., AAMFT, CFLE, Psychotherapist

"Liberating! As a father of four who has struggled for years to extricate myself
from the burden of cultural norms and conventions, Harris's book has been an
immeasurable help. I have never experienced the spirit of fatherhood as
intensely and authentically as I do now. As a general internist, I have
recommended *The Father Quest* to many of my patients who have come to me
with depression, looking for help and guidance."

—Joseph M. Kovaz, M.D., Internist

"This is a book to be read slowly and mused over. It is not a how-to road map on fathering, but rather guideposts to broaden our understanding and help us determine what is significant to us. As Harris says, 'A great deal of the journey to the FATHER is individual inner work.' The book's ability to meet us where we are allows it to be read and reread at a later time and a deeper level."

—J. Timothy May, Divisional President, May Apparel Co.

"This book is practical, probing, and inspiring as it leads into a rich contextual framework for understanding the meaning of fatherhood and fathers—a meaning that is passionately important to all of us as individuals and to the healing of our culture. I recommend this book to women and men who are seeking to understand their lives and grow into a sense of wholeness."

—Linda A. van Dyck, M. Div., Jungian Analyst

"In *The Father Quest,* Bud Harris has carried forward the pioneering work of C.G. Jung in understanding the role of Father in our society and the world. Following Eric Neumann's example of clarifying Jung's work for a broader audience, Harris has brought candor and sensitivity to his theory of "the Father." He reminds in the face of present-day writers who condemn the father principle, citing the misuse and excesses of the patriarchal powers, that the spirit of fatherhood first calls us… to become competent participants in the world of the living… to dream, grow, and create [and] to find the unforeseen potential that lurks within all of us, and bring it forth with strength and purpose, in a manner that substantiates ourselves and contributes to culture."

—Battle Bell, Jungian Analyst

"Most of us have been inadequately prepared to fulfill our roles as fathers. Family violence and absent fathers haunt our headlines, reminding us of our inadequacies. Bud Harris gives us a model for developing a deeper under-standing of our roles as fathers. Going even deeper, he helps us realize how an understanding of the family role can prepare us for the greater challenge of fulfilling our potential in life. This book is a fascinating guide into the meaning of fatherhood."

—John G.B. Ellison, Jr., C.E.O., Ellison Company

"A deep and penetrating look into the manifestations of the lost, absent, or decayed father in our culture. Harris challenges us to open our hearts to the guiding principles of father and fatherhood in *The Odyssey.* Here is a plea to put aside easy answers and, with steadfast striving, regain the forgotten images necessary to embrace life with open arms and live passionately the essence of fatherhood."

—Janet S. Hampton, M.S., Psychotherapist

This book has been donated by
Dean Frantz
and
Friends of Jung in Fort Wayne

THE
FATHER QUEST

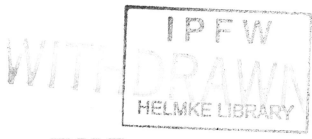

THE
FATHER QUEST

Rediscovering An
Elemental Psychic Force

Bud Harris

ALEXANDER BOOKS
65 Macedonia Road
Alexander, North Carolina 28701

Publisher: Ralph Roberts
Vice-President/Operations: Pat Hutchison Roberts

Editors: Ralph Roberts, Pat Hutchison Roberts, Gayle Graham

Cover design: Mark Wilson and **WorldComm**®
Cover and interior art: Tom Schulz
Cover photograph: Livio Piatti
Interior design & electronic Page Assembly: **WorldComm**®
Indexing: The Roberts Group

10   9   8   7   6   5   4   3   2   1

Library of Congress Cataloging-in-Publication

Harris, Clifton Tumlin Bud, 1937—
      The father quest   :   rediscovering an elemental psychic force /
      C.T.B. "Bud" Harris.
               p.   cm.
      Includes bibliographical references and index
      ISBN 1-57090-035-3 (alk. paper)
        1. Fatherhood--Psychological aspects.   2. Father and child.
      3. Parenting.   I. Title
      HQ756.H367   1996
      306.874'2--dc20   96-1531
                                           CIP

Alexander Books—a division of Creativity, Inc.—is a full–service publisher located at 65 Macedonia Road, Alexander NC 28701. Phone (704) 252–9515, Fax (704) 255–8719. For orders only: 1-800-472-0438. Visa and MasterCard accepted.

Alexander Books is distributed to the trade by Midpoint Trade Books, Inc., 27 West 20th Street, New York NY 10011, (212) 727-0190, (212) 727-0195 fax.

Acknowledgments

Every effort has been made to trace all copyright holders but if any has been inadvertently overlooked, the author and publisher will be pleased to make the necessary arrangement at the first opportunity.

Excerpts from Favorite Folk Tales from Around the World by Jane Yolen, editor Introduction, Introductory material and Notes © 1986 by Jane Yolen, Compilation © 1986 by Random House, Inc. Reprinted by permission of Pantheon Books, a division of Random House. Inc.

Lyrics from "Only the Good Die Young," Seventh Son of a Seventh Son (Harris/Dickinson) by Iron Maiden reprinted by permission of Sanctuary Music Management Ltd.

Excerpts from C. G. Jung, Collected Works (Princeton, NJ.: Princeton University Press) reprinted by permission of the publisher.

Both of my parents circulate in my blood... I have carried them all of my days; neither has died. As long as I live, they too will live inside me and battle in their antithetical ways to govern my thoughts and actions. My lifelong effort is to reconcile them... to make the discord between them, which breaks out incessantly within me, turn to harmony inside their son's heart.

—*Nikos Kazantzakis*

For :

Bud Harris, Senior

Bill Curry, Senior

and

"Doc" McKay, Senior

CONTENTS

Introduction

As our interest in personal development and other related topics (such as the abuse in families) continues to grow, we find that a number of questions are coming up about fathers and fatherhood. Many people feel wounded by the presence of their father or by the lack of his presence. We may end up asking ourselves: "Who was he?" "Do I miss him?" or "How much should I miss him?" As a man, I may wonder how I can be a good father. A woman may wonder what kind of father her children really have.

Fathers today, especially those with adolescents, are finding themselves particularly perplexed. While fathers probably have been flabbergasted by adolescents since the beginning of time, our world seems to plunge us beyond a simple feeling of bewilderment into fear and even desperation. The tremendous dangers adolescents can get into so quickly—drugs, disease, auto accidents, and so forth—are enough in themselves to scare us to death. But then there are the more sophisticated problems such as eating disorders or teen suicide that are now nationwide.

But even those who are not fathers are finding they need to understand fatherhood. Whether fathers are absent, present, ignored, intimidating, or wimps, we are beginning to see once again that their influence flows throughout the life of each of us. From birth until death, the image of *father* forms one of the great cornerstones of our personalities. And in a world of two-income families, single-parent families, institutional child rearing, and feminism, we can rightfully ask if the image of father is dead or alive. As sexual and social roles have shifted, fatherhood seems to have slipped into some type of unconscious twilight zone.

To pull this image back into focus, we must try to understand the deeper meanings of fatherhood. Without this deeper understanding, we can fall into the modern psychological trap of treating the symptoms through popular psychological techniques. These practical techniques deal with problems in parenting, communication, aging, grief, conflict resolution, and so on. While often helpful on an outer or social level, they do little to deepen our engagement with ourselves and with life in general. Unless we find the deeper meanings of fatherhood, we will become stuck in our efforts to deal with symptoms rather than attack the source of our dis-ease itself. Certainly fathers—all men—need to understand fatherhood. But the fact is, as the following example will show, all *people* need to understand fatherhood.

One of my analysands is the divorced mother of two teenage sons. She recently told me of an interesting little experiment she conducted with some other women about their fathers. She had been examining the effects her father had on her development and decided to ask a number of women on different levels in her organization whether their fathers ever made them feel pretty and/ or intelligent. She found that women whose fathers let them know they were attractive still felt attractive whether they were or not, and women whose fathers made them feel intelligent still felt intelligent whether they were or not.

Fathers and even masculinity in general are just as important to women as they are to men. Fathers affect daughters and wives deeply in their inner development just as mothers affect sons and husbands. The father image in our culture plays an important part in everyone's inner journey. To that end, this book is divided into two sections, the first reflects on what fatherhood has been in the past. Often a look at our history can show us what it means to be human. Repeatedly, we find that some ancient ancestor did the essential things in life naturally—in the language of depth psychology, unconsciously—essential things that we have forgotten through centuries of inattention and distortion. As modern life developed, many of the structures that made us who we are have faded into the mists of time, or in the internal sense, into the mists of our personal and collective unconscious minds.

One way to recover these structures is to look at myths and rituals. Myths order human experience by providing a vision of the underlying structure of reality. When these myths are forgotten, our lives become shallow, fragmented, and chaotic. The images these myths contained do not die–they cannot die because they offer us the only point of departure for psychological and spiritual renewal. According to Jungian psychology, these images go underground instead, concealing themselves within our ordinary lives. To find them again we have to work our way back to the source and rediscover the meanings in the faded myths. We have to *reawaken* our imagination, the treasure of images within us, and to search out and contemplate these images in order to assimilate them into our lives. To imagine is to make bridges between mind and body, spirit and nature, and ourselves and the universe. When we lack imagination, the metaphors that inform our lives fade away. Without our metaphors we are left with rules–skeletons stripped of the flesh of meaning.

When our imaginations are working and we can see the everyday as metaphor, we no longer need the rules. The deeper meaning that the metaphors bring to light make the essential things in life self-evident. Once again, we can return to our imagination and play let's pretend. Paradoxically, we can become better fathered by touching the imaginative world of childhood and its essential potentials and possibilities. In the process, we will discover that the metaphors of fatherhood apply to much more than simple flesh and blood fathers, either our fathers or ourselves as fathers. Men and women throughout history have developed culture, which makes us, in a certain sense, the parents of our society for better or worse. In the upcoming chapters, I will capitalize "Fatherhood" to distinguish cultural fatherhood–our obligation to be a father to culture and society–from personal fatherhood.

There are even deeper meanings to fatherhood. Beginning with the ancient cave drawings, humankind has envisioned elemental images beyond our everyday experience. This notion faded briefly in the 18th and 19th centuries as rationalism invaded science, only to return in full force in the scholarship and science of this century. These elemental images are what Jung referred to as the archetypes, the originals beyond our experience whose energy renews the substance of life and formats its course. These images live in the human psyche and merge to inform our imaginations, and indirectly give shape to many of our actions and experiences. Our natural fathers and ourselves as fathers only reflect a small portion of that larger archetype within our psyche. Throughout the book I will use all capitals to refer to these archetypal images, such as FATHER, REALITY, or AUTHORITY.

Beyond this elemental image lies an even greater one, unseen and calling us into the mists of an unseeable future, beyond ourselves–beyond our own self-image and beyond the petty show of our existence. I refer to the image of this elemental force in the psyche of humanity the Transcendent FATHER or the GREAT FATHER.

Then, once the first part of this book has unearthed the essential foundation stones of fatherhood, the second part will put in place a few more building blocks drawn from my studies, clinical and personal experience. With this foundation and the suggestion of some directions, I hope you will build your own model of fathering. I also hope you will go a step further and develop your own notion of the place of the father and the FATHER archetype within yourself and within your version of the story of humanity.

A final word of warning. Mircea Eliade[1] points out that

> *"... history does not radically modify the structure of an 'imminent' symbolism. History continually adds new meanings to it, but these do not destroy the structure of the symbol."*

The ancient meanings of archetypes are in a sense permanent. They must simply be rediscovered, renewed, and lived by each generation. And how we live out the metaphors of our myths determines the shape of our culture.

But a new element now characterizes the images surrounding the FATHER archetype. That element is that we must now understand and assimilate consciously and individually what was once less conscious and societal. We cannot go back to the old ways.

The personal histories I describe in this book represent real-life experiences, but I have altered some details and occasionally made composites of individual cases to disguise the identity of any one person. Any similarity between these illustrations and an actual family or person is purely coincidental.

PART 1:

CORNERSTONES

1

Fatherhood: An Image Lost, A Challenge Discovered

Dad! You better give me something. You better give me something fast...Dad, stand up for me.

—James Dean, *Rebel Without a Cause*

In the report of his travels throughout America in the 1840s Alexis de Tocqueville noted how close fathers and sons were. They appeared to work together, fight together, and support each other in the enterprise of developing a new country. He even suggested that European fathers and sons could learn from Americans. A few generations later, in the 1950s, we find a very different scene as James Dean had to beg his father for simple recognition. Adolescents today are still begging and Dad has grown more elusive than ever. Is fatherhood dead or alive in America?

For centuries, children peering through the mists of childhood, saw their fathers as gods. Not surprising, since for centuries fathers received their authority from God, reinforced and inspired through the patriarchal institutions of king, state, and church. Every father could think of himself as a "king in his own castle" because there were real kings in real castles. Now this once powerful image has turned into a caricature. The king in his castle is Archie Bunker. Dagwood, the pattern for several generations of comic-strip, radio and TV sitcom fathers, leaves the castle for work every morning and spends much of his time at home napping on the couch. The once powerful character of father is absent, figuratively or literally, in many modern homes.

So it's not surprising that we hear daily from new directions that the place in the human spirit reserved for fathers is vacant.

This absence results in what psychologists call de-individualized sons. De-individualization is the state of alienation a boy develops when he doesn't have a father to identify with and then rebel against. De-individualized men have trouble relating as adults to other adults and particularly to their own wives and children. They may strive to become the man their father was not, creating grandiose ideals or embracing macho images to compensate for the lack of real masculinity in their development. Or they may become passive, unable to initiate their own lives, and bedeviled by a sense of unworthiness, that floods their souls at the slightest crisis. The meaning that could sustain their life seems to have quietly leaked out while they weren't looking. Wounded sons often succumb to mother and end up spending their lives seeking direction and approval—often their very identities—from women and institutions and devoting their lives in return to pleasing them.

The breakdown of fatherhood also produces wounded daughters. One way or another, all women become father's daughters. If Dad is absent, emotionally or otherwise, then a woman's early idealizations and longings will last into adulthood without being tempered by reality. She will have trouble relating to men. She will long for a relationship deeply, on the one hand, and yet will idealize it so strongly that there is little hope of it being humanly possible. Often the problem will be compounded, for she will find herself being attracted to men who aren't capable of self-responsibility and intimacy.

Many such women so idealize the man's world that they become daughters of the patriarchy seeking inner security through either professional or social achievement or rebellion against the system in alternate lifestyles. Success in either direction leaves such women feeling like imposters. Men seem either godlike and omnipotent or weak and undependable, or both. Often the anger is easier to see in women than in men, but there's a deep fury and grief in both of them. Their anger and grief may take many self-destructive forms—depression, suicide, addictions, or promiscuity to name a few. Self-destruction and self-hate commonly creep in when our need to love and be loved is sealed away in some inner cavern. Children who cannot identify with their parents often end up identifying with their parents' pathologies.

On the collective level, a society without fathers loses the father qualities it needs to pursue long-term commitments. Our government can't ask citizens to sacrifice in order to pursue goals of character and compassion. And many of the adolescent problems that gain so much media attention—from the decline in education to the rise in drug use—reflect a society that cannot guide youth into self-responsible adulthood.

As the status of father has declined, some have wondered if women, buoyed by the feminist movement, have moved in to assume the father's authority. While this situation may be the case in some modern families, I have consistently found in the families I've worked with that the position of the mother has become almost as impossible as that of the father. Nevertheless, I think it's fair to say that the rhetoric against our patriarchal heritage has contributed to the decline in the role of paternal authority, in general.

One result of this rhetoric is the emergence of a new kind of father, the nurturing father. Often, this father is the safe, sensitive, expressive man that some feminists suggest all men should become. But I wonder whether this man is just our New Age "soft-male" turned father, and if so, will he have the other qualities needed to be a father? Society has labeled the old father an absolute monarch who cared a great deal about maintaining his authority and little about intimacy—Archie relaxing in his chair while Edith brought him his slippers. And there is some truth in this picture. Our competitive culture has infected many men with an excessive drive for power so that it is easier for them to thrust themselves into a career than to pursue the perilous path toward intimacy.

Life Today: Finding the Creative Choice

Technology and the industrial-marketing revolution have dramatically changed the relationship of the father to his family. De Tocqueville described an America where fathers and sons worked side by side and boys learned how to be men by being with men. But if we examine it a little more closely, we find that de Tocqueville's America was an exception, if not an idealization. Throughout the centuries men frequently have been absent from home—going on hunts, going to war, going on adventures and spiritual quests—and the search for the missing father has been an eternal psychological task represented in myths and legends throughout history.

Jim was a physician in his early forties. He had reached a point where his practice was substantial and he earned a comfortable living. He had been born into the family of blue-collar, middle-class parents. For as long as he could remember, his father had been distant, and his mother depressed. His parents had structured their lives around the institutional instruction and the conventional values of their church. In a flare of adolescent energy and creativity, Jim had burst his familial bonds and gone to medical school, thereby achieving a life beyond his parents' understanding. As the years passed, however, their temperament and values slowly resurfaced in his personality. In spite of his success, he had become rigid, dogmatic, pessimistic, and distant from his children.

Jim became aware of his emotional state through the ensuing depression that brought him into analysis. During this period, he dreamed that he was in the ocean with his seventeen-year-old son and his father. His son was holding on to one of his arms and his father to the other. As they descended, he was seized with panic because he was drowning and could not make them realize it. After telling me the dream, he observed that his son was applying to colleges and was expecting him to pay his way to an expensive school. Jim also was thinking about making some changes to enliven his life that might reduce his income for a while. As we deliberated on the images of this dream, he recognized that each figure symbolized a set of "obligations" and "responsibility" that were drowning him. I went a step further and noted that three generations of men were present and they were in the sea. This combination of men, generations, and the sea reminded us of the *Odyssey* and I suggested he read it. As he studied it over a period of weeks, new doors began to open in his mind. He felt "released" and allowed fresh alternatives to come into his perceptions. In addition, he began to mourn for his own lost youth and to realize how desperate his flight into achievement and adjustment had been as he had tried to forge his identity.

The transformational powers of such stories can often help us and *The Odyssey* is one of the earliest ones about fathers. Let's pause for a moment and take a brief look at it and how it can help guide us into the issues throughout this book. I hope that you will go beyond my summary and carefully study the myth as Jim did.

Myths are far older than the science of psychology, and for many generations have been guiding elders to a developing humanity. They require that we participate in them by giving them our conscious attention and, if we can open our hearts to them, we find they will challenge us to a deeper understanding of ourselves and a more vital engagement with life.

As we study myths, the stories that have never been in fact but are always happening, we begin to realize that many of the problems we face also have "always been." Today they are simply clothed in the appearances of our time. Such is the case in our search for the Father. As Jim studied the many struggles in *The Odyssey*, he discovered this nature of mythology. Their themes offer a primordial structure that can bring a sense of order and centering to our search. *The Odyssey*, told by Homer and carried to us over thousands of years, has become elementary in our heritage. It is a tale of a son's search for his father, his father's search for home and reconciliation with his own father.

In the opening lines of the epic, Homer invokes our interest and asks us to join in full participation, intellect (words), and emotions (music) in a relationship with the muse that may give birth to inspiration and unity. He then asks the muse to help us understand this story in our time.

The Odyssey — A Quest for Maturity and Wholeness

A Summary and Commentary:[1] Homer's great epic of the Trojan War, *The Iliad*, preceded his tale that we know as *The Odyssey*. As *The Iliad* unfolds, we are introduced to the perspective that the human and the divine interact through dreams, oracles, and inspirational visions. As the ten-year Trojan War progresses, we find that the most heroic warriors on both sides are killed. As the war ends, the victorious Greeks still face long and perilous voyages home. Their returns have become precarious, because they have offended a number of the gods during the war. Many of them encounter tragic and arduous journeys home as a result of their offenses.

Of the returning group, Odysseus was destined to wander the longest. He struggled with the worlds of humans and the supernatural for another ten years before reaching home.

As *The Odyssey*, the story of his return home, begins, all the survivors of the war reach home except for Odysseus. On Mount Olympus, Zeus, the lord of earth and sky and the father god of the Greeks, is conducting a council of the gods. He is interrupted by Athene, the goddess who protects heroes and personifies courage and wisdom. She reminds Zeus of Odysseus' stagnated journey and demands the gods help him in spite of Poseidon's anger toward him. Poseidon, the turbulent sea god, is angry with Odysseus for blinding one of his sons.

During the time of the council, Odysseus is being held captive by the nymph, Calypso, who wishes to marry him. Athene suggests that Zeus and his messenger, Hermes, free Odysseus while Athene visits Odysseus' son, Telemachus, who is at home with his mother. From this point on, the first four books in the epic are concerned with Telemachus and his search for his father.

Dressed as a mighty warrior, Athene travels to Ithaca, Odysseus' homeland where she finds a state of chaos. Penelope, Odysseus' wife, has spent the passing years patiently and faithfully awaiting her husband's return. During this time, a number of petty princes and noblemen have shown up at her home. Officially they were there to court her, but they were also depleting Odysseus' estate with prolonged feasts and parties. Paradoxically, the kingdom seems to belong to Penelope. Neither Odysseus' son, Telemachus, nor his father, Laertes, can assert themselves and assume the kingship while Odysseus is absent. The suitors are there because if Odysseus is declared dead, whoever Penelope chooses to marry will become the new king. It appears that Penelope has the right of ownership but cannot wield authority over it.

Changing her appearance, Athene approaches Telemachus in the guise of Mentes, an old friend of his father. She advises him that his father is still alive, and he tells her about the problems of his mother and the kingdom. In response, she instructs him to undertake a search for his father. She also informs him that if Odysseus is dead, then it is time for him to face his own responsibilities. After a dream foretelling his intended journey, Telemachus gives up his sorrowful state and begins to act. He assembles his mother's suitors and announces his intention to both search for his father and to punish them for their wastefulness. They react aggressively to his assertions and another old friend of his father, Mentor, rises to his support. Athene then begins taking on the appearance of Mentor as she helps Telemachus prepare for his trip and evade the angry suitors.

Telemachus, guided by Athene as Mentor, begins his travels by visiting King Nestor, the oldest and the wisest of the Greeks at Troy, and a former friend of his father. Nestor suggests that Telemachus consult Menelaus, who may have more recent information about his father. Menelaus was the king of Sparta, and it was his wife, Helen, the most beautiful woman in the world, who had precipitated the Trojan War. With appropriate sacrifices to Athene, Nestor helps Telemachus on his way.

Menelaus was shocked at Telemachus' story about his homeland. He also tells of his own adventures on his voyage home. Meanwhile, the suitors discover the absence of Telemachus and plot to ambush him upon his return. Penelope, learning of her son's journey, is overcome by grief and worry, but during the night, Athene comforts her with a reassuring dream.

In this episode, Menelaus and Helen seem more like a conventional old couple than the passionate warring king and beautiful queen whose involvement caused so many worlds to crumble. While journeying to consult with Nestor and then Menelaus and Helen, Telemachus is introduced to a whole new world of experience and perspective. By now he is far from the isolated comfort of his sheltered life on the island of his mother. He has begun the journey that will result in his recognition as a man by gods and mortals.

Once again Athene raises the issue of Odysseus during a divine assembly, and Zeus finally agrees to send Hermes to instruct Calypso to release him. Bitterly, Calypso accedes to Zeus and helps Odysseus depart. Seeing Odysseus again at sea, Poseidon grows angry and causes a violent storm. It is only with Athene's help through great danger and suffering that he reaches the island of the Phaeacians where he falls into an exhausted sleep among the olive branches.

At this point in the story, Odysseus begins to reflect a character with more depth and complexity than was previously shown in *The*

Iliad. We begin to see him as a man possessed by a contradictory set of motives. He clearly enjoys the adventurous life of the wanderer while also longing for home. As a hero he is able to live by his intellect as well as by his strength and courage, and his code of conduct is anything but rigid. He retains a realistic concept of self-interest and his ultimate goals.

Awakening exhausted and starving, Odysseus is discovered by Princess Nausicaa of Phaeacia and her attendants. She brings him to the palace of her parents, King Alcinous and Queen Arete, where he is treated with great kindness and hospitality. When the queen questions him as to his identity, he evades her and speaks of his skills as a sailor before being caught in the terrible storm that washed him ashore. As part of his hospitality, a strong and sacred tradition in that time, King Alcinous calls for a large celebration and summons a famous bard to perform for the gathering. The king informs the crowd that he is unable to name his guest, and Odysseus refuses to be recognized.

The messages of the bard, however, catch Odysseus unaware. The bard presents compelling stories of the siege of Troy that include poignant moments from Odysseus' experience. While he is moved to tears, his identity continues to be a secret, for the story is moving to everyone in the assembly. Following the bard's performance in these celebrations, games were customarily held. At this point an insolent guest taunts Odysseus, claiming that he must be soft, perhaps a merchant or an accountant. To everyone's surprise, Odysseus straightens his frame that has been bent by exhaustion and reveals the body of a powerful athlete. Even without a name, his body and skill slowly begin to reveal his identity during the games.

After the games, the bard begins to sing again. Odysseus asks him to sing about the Trojan horse. He alone, at this point, knows that he is the hero of this story. But the bard is so skillful in weaving the song that Odysseus is caught, transfixed between his experience and the story, between his deception and his identity. To unravel this entanglement requires the truth of his experience and the persuasion of the story teller. Odysseus' emotions cling to the way in which the singing of the bard knits events together. After this event, Odysseus himself must recognize, must own his identity and the connection between his being and his history. As his past becomes alive in his memory, it is no longer just a series of events, but a story with an origin. The question of a story and an origin evokes a longing for a solution and leads him back to his quest for his homeland.

His past is no longer just a series of events or successive heroic tasks. It has become an unbroken thread leading back to his beginnings and his parents, the authors of his name. No longer able to manipulate his story to his own advantage, he finds himself seized by it and is once again its subject. Paradoxically, and at his own request, the bard has caught Odysseus in his art and has woven his inner and outer worlds together, bringing about a reintegration of his personality and an acceptance of himself as once again his name becomes explicit. Odysseus' personal unity has returned through an outside source and a relationship to circumstances and other people captured in the song of the bard.

King Alcinous again asks his name. At this point Odysseus reveals his name and proceeds to tell them the tale of his adventures. This recitation is the final step in bringing his recent experiences into the storyline that is making up the progress of his development and the thread of his destiny. The king had pointed out that nobody has ever lived without a name, but Odysseus had played a painful and deceptive game by naming himself "Nobody." As his story unfolds, we can see how this game concretely saved his life while simultaneously expressing the deeper truth of an inner self being torn asunder.

Odysseus begins his tale as he and his men leave Troy bound for home. Early in their journey they stop to raid the land of the Cicones. After an initial success, they suffer from a frightful counterattack and suffer many casualties before escaping. While battling the Cicones, they spare a priest of Apollo (the god of intellect, music, and proper proportions in the flow of life). In return he gives them a fragrant red wine, which saves them in their encounter with Polyphemus. This incident helps us remember that a connecting thread binds each episode of his adventures into a tapestry of destiny.

The Greeks sail on through a vicious storm until they reach the land of the Lotus Eaters, who seemed friendly. But the Greeks who ate the fruit of the lotus soon lost their memories of home and responsibility, and wanted to remain in this enraptured state.

Odysseus and those who were not affected had great difficulty rescuing their comrades and setting sail once more.

Odysseus and his men then arrive at the island of the Cyclops, a land that appears fertile and rich. Driven by curiosity and greed, he leads a scouting party inland. They discover a cave outfitted for a shepherd where they begin to feast and await its occupant. Soon enough he returns and seals the cave. The Greeks discover that they have been captured by a one-eyed monster, the Titan Polyphemus, a son of Poseidon. Polyphemus immediately ate two of the Greeks for supper.

Terrorized by the vicious power of Polyphemus and their deadly predicament, Odysseus is forced to rely on his shrewd intelligence and his ability to be deceptive. He gives some of the wine from the priest of Apollo to Polyphemus, making him drunk. He tells the giant that his name is "Nobody" and in gratitude for the excellent wine, the giant said that he would eat him last. Then Odysseus and his men blinded the giant with a sharpened pole while he was in a drunken sleep.

Polyphemus cried out in agony. When the other Cyclops came running to the cave's entrance, he screamed, "Nobody is killing me." They assumed either not much was wrong or the problem was caused by a god and they couldn't help. Then as Polyphemus let his sheep out of the cave to pasture, counting them by touch, Odysseus and his men escaped by clinging to the sheep's underbellies. As Odysseus sailed away, he yelled his true name and the Cyclops almost destroyed him by hurling the top of a mountain at him. Polyphemus prayed to his father, Poseidon, that Odysseus' voyage be long and filled with distress, that his companions be lost, and that upon his arrival he would discover trouble at home. His prayer was heard, and the thread of the tale continued.

Odysseus and his men sail on to many other adventures. Each adventure ends with an apparent escape that turns out to be a further seeking. His fleet reaches the floating island of Aeolus who gives the Greeks a bag containing all of the winds, and shows them which one to release in order to reach home. Odysseus is almost home when he allows his vigilance and discipline to lapse, and he falls asleep. His men, seized by greed, think the bag is filled with gold which he is hiding. They open it and allow the unfavorable natural forces to rush out. The ships are blown back to where they began, Aeolus' island. He refuses to help them again, supposing that the gods must be against them.

They arrive next at the land of the Laestrygonians, who sink all the Greek ships, but Odysseus' own, and eat the crews. Odysseus continues on in his solitary ship. He reaches the Island of the Dawn, which is the home of the sorceress Circe, the daughter of the sun and aunt of the other great enchantress of Greek legend, Medea. Circe turned the men in the exploring party into swine. When he finds out about their predicament, Odysseus sets out alone to rescue them. Along the way he encounters Hermes, who gives him the black and white herb Moly to protect himself and instructs him to approach Circe with his sword, threatening her, but doing no actual violence. Odysseus follows Hermes instructions, and his men are returned to human form.

Odysseus remains with Circe for a year. Finally, homesick and urged on by his men, he decides to resume his journey and Circe agrees to help him. She advises him to visit the underworld and consult with the ancient blind seer, Teiresias, to find out the difficulties he must face and how to placate Poseidon.

While there, Odysseus encounters his mother and many notable figures from his past. These experiences forge a reconnection with his ancestry and his history, which serve to deepen and transform the nature of his evolving identity. In mythic lore, these visits to the underworld are decisive steps in the reeducation of the hero, representing the rebirth of a deepened personality.

With his new knowledge, Odysseus returns to Circe and she instructs him as to how he may safely get past the enticing Sirens. Nearing the island of the Sirens, he has his men fill their ears with wax, for the singing of the Sirens lures sailors to their death on the rocks. He has himself bound to the mast so he might hear their song and survive. Once past this danger, the ship must pass between two wandering rocks in a strait that contains the twin monsters, Scylla and Charybdis. He sails too close to the cave of Scylla, who snatches six men from his ship and eats them. The otherwise safe passage through these two tests shows that Odysseus has been transformed by his experiences and that he is following the thread leading toward the reunification of his personality in the land of the Phaeacians.

The island of Thrinacia, where the sun god Helios pastures his herds of cattle and sheep, is the final stop in the journey of Circe's instruction. She has carefully admonished Odysseus not to touch a single one of these animals. Once again, Odysseus is unable to control his men and, driven by hunger, they slaughter some of the cattle while he sleeps. Helios complains to Zeus about the violation of his sacred herd. As a punishment, Zeus destroys the Greek ship with a thunderbolt during a storm, killing all of them but Odysseus. Odysseus then drifts back to the whirlpool of Charybdis, where he narrowly avoids death and finally drifts on to the island of Calypso. When he is released from this island by the gods intervention, he sets sail on a raft only to be wrecked in another storm unleashed by Poseidon. From this experience, he is flung ashore on the island of the Phaeacians. It is here that he eventually reveals his name to King Alcinous and tells the story of his adventures. It is during this time of remembrance that the patterns of his life begin to take form and the deeper nature of his challenges is revealed.

The Phaeacians are generous and give Odysseus many gifts and transport back to Ithaca. He reaches his homeland ten years after the fall of Troy and on another ship, as Polyphemus had prayed. But Poseidon's hostility remains unsatisfied, and as the Phaeacians return home, he turns their ship and crew to stone in their own harbor.

Athene meets Odysseus on the beach of his homeland. There she confronts his duplicity and admonishes him not to play that game with her. Then she disguises him as a beggar and sends him to the home of the swineherd, Eumaneus, for shelter. Athene has set up the drama of his return to be played out between the outer layer of appearances and the inner layer of his true identity. It is a painful split, for as he encounters old friends, he cannot reveal himself and put an end to their grief. He must go along with their assumption that he is dead, splitting the living from the dead until he can reclaim his rightful place, that is, to start living again as his true self. He tells a story to those he meets which gives evidence that Odysseus is alive and also reveals the nested dimensions of the inner and outer worlds in this epic of Homer.

Athene also has sent Telemachus to the hut of Eumaneus, and here he encounters his father. At this point, two dimensions of the epic, Telemachus' quest for his father and manhood, and Odysseus' quest for his homeland, his kingship and reconcilia-

tion come together into a single story. Telemachus has under-
gone an initiation into his first maturity, the maturity of a
substantial personality. Odysseus has journeyed through the
initiation into a second maturity, that of depth and a relationship
with the truth of himself and life.

In a touching scene, Telemachus has difficulty believing that
this person is his father, a man that he can embrace and not some
god playing a trick on him. Odysseus confronts his son, arguing that
he is not the god that Telemachus thinks he is, but his father. Then
they embrace and weep. This scene is both touching and important,
and I will discuss it further in later chapters.

After their reconciliation, father and son plan how to rid their
land of the suitors. Then Odysseus goes to the palace still disguised
as a beggar. While there, he is recognized by his old dog, Argos,
who then dies. The suitors treat the beggar with derision and
Penelope, out of compassion, asks him to her room in order to
inquire about her husband. He maintains his disguise and invents
a tale of many hardships in which he has occasionally encountered
her husband. Later in the evening, Penelope's sleep is troubled as
a result of the conversation and she prays to Artemis, a protector of
the feminine. Odysseus is visited by Athene, and he prays to Zeus.
Carefully, he watches his servants and old friends to see who
remains faithful. Telemachus awaits his father's signal to act.
Thunder rumbles, giving divine support to Odysseus' plans and
divine sanction to the coming bloodbath. A feeling of impending
doom permeates this portion of the epic.

Penelope has told Odysseus that on the following day she will
accept as her husband whoever can string Odysseus' bow, and
shoot an arrow through twelve axe heads in a line. The bow is one
of those marvelous weapons that only the appropriate hero can
wield. None of the suitors can string it. Telemachus makes three
attempts and probably will succeed on the fourth, but his father
stops him. This scene represents another turning point, for father
and son are not in competition. Who is the strongest is not a
question, for they need each other. Finally the beggar, with
Telemachus' support, tries the bow. He strings it easily and reveals
his true identity by shooting an arrow through the twelve axe heads.

Telemachus steps to his father's side, and they kill all the suitors
and the servants who had been unfaithful, sparing only a poet. Once

he has cleaned his house and put it in order, Odysseus approaches Penelope in her chamber. Their reconciliation is lovely. However, she is slow to believe that it is really him. To convince her, he has to explain the secret construction of their bed. This image is one of a concentric structure, a closed-in circle symbolizing wholeness within a protected inner space.

Odysseus is reunited with his people through the recognition of a scar on his leg. When young, he had been injured while hunting a boar with his maternal grandfather and uncles. His old nurse, Eurycleia, recognized the wound and articulated his identity. Once again the importance of the maternal genealogy is emphasized.

In the final scenes of the epic, Odysseus returns to his father's house and identifies himself. The aging man greets him with touching joy. Meanwhile, the relatives of the slain suitors have started a civil war. The three reconciled generations of men stand side by side to meet their angry antagonists. Zeus decides that the actions of Odysseus were justified and gives his daughter a free hand to restore order on Ithaca. She intervenes and orders the conflict concluded. Once again in the guise of the wise old man, Mentor, she establishes peace and Odysseus reigns as king.

By the time we finish carefully reading this story, it becomes easy to realize that these troubled journeys are through the waters of our own psychological development. Again and again escapes become new searches. The necessary mistakes or blunders are made that seem to plunge the heroes into disaster but, in fact, plunge them further into the transformational powers of their journeys and, finally, into a profound symmetry of reconciliation.

Telemachus' quest in many ways parallels that of his father. The journey of Telemachus ends when he becomes an adult and is recognized as a man by gods and mortals. The journey of Odysseus ends when he becomes a king and takes his place with his queen in his kingdom. Odysseus' rise to his kingdom represents a man's spiritual and psychological development in the second half of his psychological life, after he has established his adult identity as Telemachus did. The feminine principle is woven into both of these tales in beautiful symbolic form—Athena guides Telemachus in the form of the wise old man Mentor, and Odysseus joins his queen as a mature king only after many perilous adventures with the women, nymphs, and goddesses who represent his feminine side.

This tale and others show that the quest for the absent father is as old as time. This problem is an *archetypal* issue. Father, on any psychological level, is rarely close by. Every man must search for the father in himself over and over as he grows and matures. In fact, in most of western mythology the hero's quest begins with an absent father.

Since it is an archetypal issue, the quest for the missing father is much more than a psychological problem that afflicts only a few. The search for the FATHER is an eternal search, lived out in every generation and, in one form or another, in each person in every generation. We *all* need to seek for the archetypal attributes lost to our own experience. The purpose of the quest is not simply to solve a problem or heal a wound, but to carry forward our consciousness and culture, and to redefine the cosmos.

Since the missing father is an archetypal issue, myths, legends, and fairy tales (the conduits of human wisdom throughout the ages) can guide us in our search. This doesn't mean that they will provide us with a simple solution or literal answer. If they did, they would be limited to their own time, and the ancient Greek answer would not necessarily help a modern American. Instead, the archetypal patterns found in these tales express eternal truths that by their very nature cannot be literal truths. At best, the myths can give us the form to build on the way a sculptor makes the wire skeleton to support a clay sculpture. Each of us must make our own sculpture, molding our own experience to the archetypal form.

It is also part of our task to understand our culture well enough to utilize this ancient knowledge in our present world. The fragmented image of the FATHER in our culture is a challenge for us to raise ourselves and our society to a new level of consciousness. If we fail this challenge, we will find our society becoming increasingly fragmented.

Actually, even success can lead to fragmentation, at least temporarily. The process of fragmentation of an old image to make room for a new one is as archetypal as the search for the FATHER. Disintegration (symbolized in the myths as death) leads to a new integration and regeneration (in the myths, resurrection) in the traditional cycle of life, death, and rebirth. Psychologically, old ideas, attitudes, perspectives, and often our old identities have to die. This process involves suffering because giving up the old ways is never easy and forming a new identity is risky and painful. We cannot go through a major transition without conflict—new consciousness is only born as old values break down. Time and again, we need to betray our naive and innocent attitudes, how life should be, in order to reconnect to the eternal mystery of life as it is.

Joseph Campbell notes in *The Hero With a Thousand Faces*:

> *Whether small or great, and no matter what the stage or grade of life, the Call rings up the curtain, always, on a mystery of transformation—a rite, or a moment of spiritual passage, which, when completed, amounts to a dying and a birth. The familiar life horizon has been outgrown; the old concepts, ideals, and emotional patterns no longer fit; the time for the passing of a threshold is at hand.*[2]

The Odyssey substantiates these points. Almost every one of the twenty-four books contains a conflict of some sort, and the final reconciliation and state of peace rests upon a final bloodbath. The symbolic meaning is one of ongoing inner struggle. In addition, there is the dimension of Odysseus seeking his homeland and the necessity of his developing his identity through the story of his historic episodes. Like him, the first step in our transformation is to discover our past, since our past is always the ground of our future growth. It is our past which we rebuild as we progress through the cycles of transformation, so as we lift our level of consciousness we must remain linked with the human wisdom that still exists in our lives whether we are conscious of it or not. If we lose this link to the past, we can become subject to the restless trends and threats of a transitional age moving too fast for us. If we choose to examine our past, to face the possible fragmentation of our lives as we come face to face with the archetypes—if we decide to seek the absent FATHER—we will discover deeper values, new meaning, and a more authentic life.

2

The Chain of Suffering
and Illusions of Healing

*Every problem, therefore, brings the possibility of
widening consciousness, but also the necessity of
saying goodbye to childlike unconsciousness and
trust in nature.*

—C.G. Jung

While our society is advancing technologically, it is in many ways regressing psychologically. True, the conflict between the individual and the community, the one and the many, is as old as the story of Cain and Abel. But the conflict is sharper in America since we began as a country of individualists and are still struggling to find a way to function as a community. Many people currently think that psychology has been focused on individual and shallow fulfillment while ignoring how our behavior may affect others as well as our responsibilities to societal growth and development. Some of these people think that the human potential movement and its influence in various psychotherapies have contributed to the high divorce rate, the lapse of sexual morality, and an orientation toward greed and materialism. In other words, psychology appears to reinforce a shallow one-sided individualist tradition.

In some ways it has. But teaching someone to be a self-defined individual is often the best way to help them deal with the alienation and anxiety of modern life. However, like it or not, individuals are shaped by their culture. If we focus exclusively on the individual and fail to deal with our cultural pathologies, these pathologies will soon surface again as individual problems. The result is an endless cycle of symptoms and treatments. It is as if we had gone to the dentist with a toothache, and he gave us a shot to ease the pain without repairing the tooth.

We can note in the opening scenes of *The Odyssey* the kingdom of Ithaca was a wasteland in disarray. The dual quests of Telemachus and Odysseus, and their reconciliation with Laertes and Penelope restored balance, peace, and prosperity to the entire kingdom. This point reflects the reality that cultural change both depends upon and culminates in the collective expression of individual experience. Consequently, in this interplay the individual and society shape and form each other. Both processes need to be consciously understood or we will continue to be victimized by our own development. The father quest is both personal and archetypal, individual and collective, and will contribute greatly to societal healing and transformation if we pursue it with sufficient depth and commitment.

There have been a number of books, television shows, and workshops on finding the father, healing the father-son or father-daughter wound, getting in touch with men's grief, and so forth. Clearly, our culture is becoming aware that we have an ache in the area of FATHER. But few of these books or seminars go deep enough into the *cariousness* of the FATHER image in our culture. This isn't surprising, given the complexity of the problems and the pressure of modern living. Any number of current problems are likely to cloud our vision as we try to find and heal the decay in FATHERHOOD. To add to the confusion, some of our other wounds are closely interrelated to the FATHER wound and we must try to separate them.

The first of these problems is the wound to the feminine in our society. It is well known by now that modern culture has cut the ground out from under the great feminine principle in our personal and collective psyches. This injury has cut off both men and women from their own natures, their bodies, and the world. And women, in particular, have been separated from the ground of their being, their sexuality, and their value in society. For decades, women's magazines have been filled with articles on relationships, diets, exercise, and sexuality, illustrating how much we are suffering in these areas and continuing to fail at coming to grips with them. In addition, as a society we give little honor to parenthood. We seem to expect women to be mothers as an avocation while their true focus is to be elsewhere, and they must take care of the process of living as an afterthought. Women have become increasingly fragmented, anxious, and guilty, and men have little idea as to how to respond to our current dilemma.

One result of this wound to the feminine, is a general wound to the process of mothering. This wound is a good example of how cultural wounds become internalized as personal wounds.

Wounded mothers are less likely to give their children a sense of security in the world, and since the wound is part of the culture, these mothers never realize that they are failing to meet their children's needs. The daughters eventually grow up to be wounded mothers themselves, out of touch with the taproot of their identity. They then pass their anxieties on to their children, thus perpetuating the cultural wound.

For sons, the more anxious, hostile, remote, or unreal the mother is, the more deeply his yearning for her will clutch at his very soul. Again and again this yearning will awaken the primordial and eternal image of MOTHER within his psyche. Every thing, person, and institution that can embrace, protect, or nourish him—his university (his alma mater), his corporation, his church, his government, his wife, and even his children—will assume this maternal form.

Marriage counselors are probably most familiar with the results of wounded mothering. The man wants unconditional love, support, and sexuality. The woman wants unconditional emotional support and intimacy. Both try to manipulate the other into giving them the nurturance that will enable them to feel safe and at home in the world. Neither is able to love or be loved, and their struggles often end in dependency, anger, and bitterness. The reason the MOTHER wound often interferes with the healing of the FATHER wound is that such a primary wound can unconsciously color our entire world view. If we are unconscious of the MOTHER wound, we end up trying to use every psychological relationship to heal it. We—both as individuals and as a culture—develop a heavily sentimental regard for nurturing, a regard that can put fathers in the position of being the nurturing mothers we wished we all had experienced.

Another problem that interferes with the healing of the FA-THER wound is that pop psychology often tries to provide the same instant gratification that we have learned to expect from consumerism. Even academic psychology has fallen victim to this trend, stressing short-term techniques to deal with pain rather than long-term genuine therapy that recognizes that pain calls attention to our problems. This shallow trend approach treats an immediate emotional response as if it were a success, whether it truly is or not. As a friend of mine told me, such "successes" are like successfully rearranging the deck chairs on the Titanic.

When people try to take these shortcuts to inner healing, they usually wind up mistaking emotional reactions for true healing and growth. They go from one book to another, one workshop to another, healing the inner whatever, getting in touch with the emotion of the month, maybe even looking for their inner guide. But their breakthroughs don't lead to integration in the real world or a unified personality. In the end, the shortcuts get them nowhere.

For many these shortcuts can become an obsession. The hard work and responsibilities of ordinary life become humdrum compared to their so-called "inner-work." This compulsion to feed our woundedness with cheap emotional reactions is very close to compulsive consumerism. As Eric Hoffer said of consumerism, "You can't get enough of what you don't really need." This addictive danger also colors our view of genuine therapy. If we don't feel better immediately, we think we must be doing something wrong.

We as a society need to put aside easy answers and cheap grace in order to search for the deeper meanings surrounding fatherhood and the FATHER archetype. Only by doing so can we find an authentic and personal foundation for our development. Understanding our wounds and how they relate to our personhood is the beginning of this process. To fail in this beginning can lead us into the trap of becoming preoccupied with our problems rather than seeing that they are the road to our health and development.

Father Wounds and the Importance of Betrayal

All of us are wounded by our parents. They were human, after all, and so often failed to meet our needs and expectations. Some types of wounding are simply a part of being human—in fact, they can often help us differentiate from our parents and form our own identities. Other forms of wounding such as those from molestation or abuse are clearly pathological.

But there is a much less obvious form of wounding that arises from our parents' love and ideals. Many middle class parents still are determined to fit their families into a cultural image of success and harmony. I suspect this image was partly a compensation for the struggles of the Great Depression and World War II. Surely this trend was also a compensation for the pressure of modern society, which has isolated our families and replaced the wisdom of the grandparents with that of institutions and professional experts. If we had to move away from our families and live in the suburbs, we were going to make sure that life in the suburbs was perfect. The decade of the 1960s with its violence, assassinations, drugs, family alienations, and the Viet Nam War destroyed our sense of order and control. Our faith in our leaders, institutions, and way of life was severely damaged, and our anxiety was moved to a more abstract level of consciousness as events seemed not only beyond our control, but also beyond our comprehension.

The result of this new anxiety has been a generation of parents who, in a well-meaning way, have become obsessed with lifestyle and achievement, as illustrated by the panic adolescents and parents feel over S.A.T. scores. Morris Berman noted that signs of achievement such as test scores have become "transitional objects" in our society—our identity, self-worth, and sense of existence depend on them.

These well-meaning parents often want to give their children what their own childhood lacked, a desire that doesn't seem too bad on the surface. The problem is that what our children need is seldom what we lacked or even desired as children. The result is an endless cycle of parents doing the wrong thing with the best intentions. Our culture traps those parents into a narrow view of life, and they in turn pass this constricted view on to their children. Their need to do their best for their children (to make up for what they missed) denies their children the chance to develop their own identities and rescues them from the kinds of struggles and suffering that allows them to find out who they really are. In order to stop this cycle, we must stop, reflect, and become more conscious of what we are doing. This reflection has to be more than just rational thought. The reflective process must include our imaginations and emotions as well. It is only when we reflect with our whole beings that we can transform unconscious compulsions into conscious and purposeful values or discard them in favor of new values.

As we consider the FATHER archetype and the effect of fathers on sons and daughters, we must also consider the wounds caused by the father's betrayal. And we have to beware of the cultural ideal that good fathers never betray their children. The abusive, overbearing, or absent father betrays his children by castrating their ability to face life and leaving a hole in their psyche filled with demons.

But a good father also must betray his children. In primitive cultures, this betrayal happened when the father allowed his son to be snatched from his family by the terrifying figures of the initiators who took the young man to the initiation ceremonies. The father had to allow his children to go into the world and face its mysteries and dangers on their own. During the initiation period, the young boy-man suffered terror and ordeals, but from these ordeals, he learned courage. This betrayal by the father was the beginning of the rite of passage from childhood to adulthood as the young man's confidence in his father we replaced by his confidence in himself. Confidence that no one can take away.

3

The Meaning of Fatherhood: A Vision Obscured

Childhood is not only important because it is the starting point for possible cripplings of instinct, but also because this is the time when, terrifying or encouraging, those far seeing dreams and images come from the soul of the child, which prepare his whole destiny.

—C. G. Jung

If I had one day when I didn't feel all confused...

—James Dean, *Rebel Without a Cause*

In *The Seasons of a Man's Life*, the national bestseller of a few years ago, Daniel Levinson[1] and his colleagues tried to understand the patterns of adult male development by studying a group of men born before 1930. The authors concluded that the men developed a type of "Dream" during childhood, adolescence, and early adulthood that operated as a personal myth to give their life a sense of meaning. This dream began as a sort of vague vision of themselves in the adult world. As they matured, their dreams evolved consciously and unconsciously out of their increasing sense of self. As a personal myth, it became a sort of subjective map for their lives' course that incorporated their goals, aspirations, and values. Levinson suggested that these men either achieved, modified, or renewed their dream at mid-life.

The above process has ancient roots. We're already seen that, in the story of Telemachus and Odysseus, both men are seeking a new identity, one at early adulthood and the other at mid-life. When older men and women go through transitions, they have to attend to the eternal adolescent who lives in all of us. For such men and women, the adolescent or their adolescent period shows up in dreams. In such a case they may appear back in high school or college or with friends or family they knew as adolescents and haven't thought of since. Likewise, real adolescents have difficulty becoming adults when their parents and culture are having difficulty making the transition into mature adulthood and mid-life.

Adolescents cannot form a vision of adulthood and a personal inner myth that will carry them into it unless their parents and society can develop a map of continuing and deepening maturity. Telemachus' development into full adulthood depended on Odysseus leaving home, first to help conquer the world of men and then to undergo the perilous voyage to deeper maturity and balance—a voyage that ended in reconciliation and wholeness. We may ask ourselves, "which is more important, forming the Dream or renewing the Dream?" The answer is that this question is the wrong one to ask, for both are interdependent. However, I must note that the notion of simple renewing or revising the dream shows that we are already slipping into a shallow perspective. The undertaking of a transition at mid-life is no simple crisis. The dangerous voyage of Odysseus indicates that this transition calls for a total transformation of one's sense of self and personal destiny.

From the initiation rites of primitive tribes to the vision quests of Native Americans, forming a Dream is an important part of becoming an adult. But our culture no longer encourages the formation of Dreams. Instead, we have developed a desperate rhythm of life fed by an impulse to strive for more and more material goods—values based on buying immediate gratification. The yearning for life is crowded out by the desire for larger homes and more sophisticated stereos, and the spirit of life is simply lost. Many middle aged people today know they're dissatisfied but don't know what they're missing. And many young adults would rather live at home than give up their parents' standard of living in order to become self-reliant. None of them are forming and maintaining their dreams.

Joseph Campbell[2] pointed out that primitive tribes were often organized along age lines as well as clan formations. The age groups often had the strongest bonding and progressed through typical stages of life such as these:

1. Newborn infant
2. Infant in carrying cradle
3. Little boy or girl
4. Bigger boy or girl
5. Young adolescent
6. Developed adolescent
7. Youth or maid of marriageable age
8. Adult/married man or woman
9. Old man or woman
10. Death

Each stage in the development process was defined by special costumes bestowed in family and tribal rituals. And with the new costume came an instructive ceremony that marked the start of a new way of life apparent to all. The actual meaning of the ceremonies differs from tribe to tribe—nomadic and hunting tribes stressed individual courage, power, insight, decision making, and a personal relationship with the spiritual world. Agrarian tribes stress cooperation and group religious rites emphasizing participation in a common spiritual ground. But the stages of human growth the ceremonies marked seem common to most cultures throughout history. We can safely consider them archetypal.

Rites of passage did more than mark the milestones of primitive life. The rites served to help the tribe members mature psychologically as they matured physically. Individually they transformed consciousness. On another level they grounded the individual and the community by integrating human and cultural experiences with biological destiny. These rites embody many of the most essential paradoxes of life, including the cycles of life, death, and rebirth as well as the tension between nature and culture.

The ritual processes of primitive cultures relieved their members of the need to form a Dream such as Levinson described. By the time Homer was telling the tale of Odysseus, the paradigm for humanity's development had changed dramatically. Originally our motivation had been guided by concrete outer (archetypal) rituals. By Homer's time we had evolved to the point where this process had become, for the most part, an inner psychological process. At this turning point in human evolution Homer, the blind poet with profound inner perception, was able to penetrate into the depths of human nature and express the golden thread of human development in his poetic epics. What had been concrete had now become imaginal, expressed in the metaphors of mythology. The vision quest of developing tribes seemed to mark an in-between stage in this transition.

As primitives progressed through the stages Campbell outlined, the rites they celebrated disrupted their old social categories and encouraged them to grow. On the other hand, the rites preserved the social fabric while moving the participators through it. There were still born and died alone, but in between the rites made them members of a community that preserved its values by defining birth, the life cycle, and death. The rites gave meaning and purpose to the various stages of life.

We cannot return to the old ways. All of the great myths and rituals dealt with moving from one level of consciousness to another. But when we lose touch with the meanings of the rituals or outgrow their symbolic forms, they no longer carry forward the transformation. Even if we maintain the fading forms, they simply become ceremonies that carry little sacred or spiritual power and fail to affect our level of consciousness. The only way to move forward to a new level of cultural consciousness is to study the rituals and try to figure out how to do consciously what we once did more naturally.

The symbols and rites in primitive initiation processes, like the metaphors and images in old tales such as *The Odyssey*, give us signposts that can help us find our way through our psychological landscape. These images and rituals can guide us to forgotten dimensions of ourselves and enrich and renew us. The different perspectives of the various rituals—hunters versus farmers, for instance—reflect fragments of our own evolving natures that we need to embrace to form a more unified consciousness.

Identity Requires Societal Support

In order for the old initiation rites to be effective, the members of the primitive societies had to believe in them. In tribes that used the vision quest for men, the prevalent culture of the tribe had to believe in the power of visions and that a man's potential could be discovered and fulfilled by the individual's quest for such a vision. In masculine initiation rites, cultural expectations supplied the essential psychological force to enable the initiate to leave his old self-image in order to step forward into the new one. Psychologically, we would say that society prepared the ground of the initiate's personality to move from the domination of one archetypal pattern (child) to that of a new archetypal pattern (adult). Each level of development reflected a new dominant archetypal pattern. These rites and rituals simply do not work without the social context that prepares the individual psychologically for the next stage. Modern men and women can go through as many vision quest experiences as they want. They may gain insights, experience strong emotional reactions, and enjoy an interesting weekend. But they will not become self-responsible adults with a vision of their new lives and identities because they haven't been prepared. Society's side of the equation is not there the way it used to be.

In these primitive rites, society supported the process where the archetypes that had been projected onto the parents were internalized by the initiates. The young man became a MAN. The young woman a WOMAN. Both had internalized their own authority, sexuality, and spirituality as understood in the context of their culture. But if our culture doesn't have healthy or clear archetypal images and transitions, initiation into adulthood fails, the archetypal images are not internalized, and the authority and identity of the individual are always *out there* somewhere.

Since Joseph Campbell first went on PBS to urge people to follow their bliss, I have had a series of successful middle-aged professional men come for analysis. These highly intelligent, successful men—all fathers in my experience—realized they have missed something but have no idea how to get in touch with their bliss in order to follow it. They have little inner imagination. Their authority and identity are still *out there,* and they are mistakenly hoping to find their bliss out there as well.

In primitive societies, the initiation was something that happened inside the initiate as well as outside. Both masculine and feminine initiations commonly took place in a *sacred space,* often simply a designated hut or circle of some type. The symbolic significance of this special space was that the initiates were taken out of secular space and time. In this space the outer and inner worlds become one. The initiation also lasted as long as they took, ending only when the initiate was transformed and welcomed back into society in their new status. The initiation was a spiritual process by its very nature, neither pressured nor hurried by secular consider-ations. They varied from days to years depending upon the tribe.

By contrast, we rush our children into the secular world by abandoning them to day-care and schools. From a tender age, we institutionalize their lives, so is it any wonder that they end up with an institutional ego that feels AUTHORITY is still *out there*? Such an ego operates on a perception of what is practical—in effect, what it can get by with—rather than what is logical, moral, or spiritual.

Mircea Eliade[3] describes an initiation for women, beginning at their first menstruation, wherein they are dressed in special clothes, isolated in a dark hut in the depths of the brush, and live only on raw food. Through these experiences, generation after generation, the women acquire a sense of the spiritual meaning and deepen the dimensions of their lives. Harshly torn from the banal, secular world, they experience the sacred nature of their own fertility. The ritual shows that, on the cosmic scale, nothing is born without sacrifice and destruction, and in learning this, they learn to surren-der to and participate in the rhythms of life.

The process was not so simple for the boy, since the signs of puberty are not so dramatic as with a young girl. Both he and the society had to *intend* for him to become a man. He had to disengage from his mother and marshal the courage and energy to become a man. Often the initiators kidnapped him from his mother, his familial home, and the world of childhood. Then he had to earn the right to become a man, to be married, and to enter the culture of the Fathers.

Typically, the rite of passage began when the boy symbolically died to his old way of life. This was signified by washing, ritual cleansing, lamenting, cutting off hair, and symbolic body paintings. Then the rites of passage proceeded with such activities as ordeals, sacrifices, instruction in tribal law, lore, mysteries, history, and sexuality. When these rites were completed, the young man was recognized as being reborn as a self-responsible adult by such ceremonies as emerging through some sort of opening, naming, the presentation of salt; and sharing in a ritual feast or meal.

Sons were never initiated by their own fathers. Instead, the *culture of the Fathers* initiated them into the world of the Fathers. And from what I've seen in my own clinical experience many men today ache for more than a personal relationship with their father. They also long for a way to join in kinship with the world of the Fathers. Institutions, though patriarchal in form, cannot fill this personal need. When a Maisai youth, for instance, finished his initiation, he was more than just an adult, he was a Maisai. He embodied his heritage in a way that most modern men do not.

Courage: The Meaning of Ordeals and Suffering

The initiation ordeals of primitive times often seem cruel and repulsive to our twentieth century sensibilities, but this practical attitude ignores the meaning of suffering in the history of human experience. Today, we simply try to avoid suffering and explain it away as irrelevant–something "someone" should do something about. Once again, we have severed the roots to our own nature and are living in a state of personal and collective illusion.

Joseph Campbell[4] pointed out that the trials, tests, and ordeals the mythological hero faced did more than simply show that the hero had the "right stuff" to really be called a hero. These trials also forced the hero to focus on something larger than himself and his own survival. This inner change is truly a heroic transformation of consciousness, one that is demanded of each person who becomes a self-responsible adult. The transformation illustrated by ancient hero myths is actualized in various degrees by most of the primitive rites of passage into adulthood.

Both creation myths and initiation rituals emphasize self-discipline as a critical point of development. For initiates, this self-discipline means bringing their instincts and emotions under control when faced with the terrors of initiation. This archetypal pattern is reflected in many of the stories of mythology. Over and over in *The Odyssey*, Odysseus had to pay a heavy price for going to sleep and losing control of his men, or having an outburst of pride, greed, or curiosity. In the Sumerian myth of Inanna, we encounter a similar pattern for feminine development. As Inanna begins her journey into transformation, she must discipline herself to give up her queenly powers, her elegant appearance, and her valuable jewels. Telemachus also had to overcome his fear and go into the unknown world, seeking his father with determination and courtesy. Self-discipline is usually thought of as the beginning of self-knowledge and in most religions is the beginning of spiritual development.

From these ordeals and sufferings, *courage* emerges as the *leitmotif* of a man's life. Each transition point in our psychological maturation calls for us to return to this basic virtue first developed in the initiation rites. Aristotle pointed out that courage is the most important of all virtues because without it we cannot practice any of the others. The early Christian mystics[5] thought that the courage of the lion (symbolically the green lion) was needed for spiritual maturation—not the meekness of the lamb. And when Aleksandr Solzhenitsyn[6] gave his commencement address at Harvard over a decade ago he listed the failure of courage in the American people as one of our greatest problems.

In initiation rites, the initiated adult has experienced a fall from innocence, but has found the strength to face the reality of adult life and join in the battle of existence. While primitive people needed this courage simply in order to survive, we today need it just as strongly as we try to heal a chaotic and fragmented world. As we develop maturity, we need the courage to form our own identity and encounter the world head on. The wise old man can't just sit around pontificating. We need him to be a warrior of the spirit, able to inform youth, guide our culture, and continually reconnect us to the child within us as the grandfathers did when they played with the children and told them stories around the ancient camp fires. These patterns of courage emerge side by side in the myths of Telemachus and Odysseus, and they should do so in each of us.

Helen Luke, commenting on the courage needed for the inner journey of developing consciousness, says:

> *The long journey toward consciousness involves constant and ruthless fighting and killing; primitive man would have starved without it and man in any age who tries to avoid it in all levels is still sucking milk from his mother's breast in a state of arrested development. Any kind of pacifism that refuses all fighting is not only doomed to failure since it denies validity to one of the basic*

facts of the unconscious, but it actually breeds more and more violence, violence of an unconscious kind which kills in order to feed those hideous distortions of human nature—the pride of ego, its power and greed.[7]

For full maturity, we need to continue to develop physical, psychological, and spiritual courage throughout our lives.

Those who have gone through the terrors of an initiation rite develop the confidence of survivors. This confidence forms the foundation of their adult personalities. They know that if they persevere, even when afraid, they will make it through their ordeals. They have the courage to endure in the face of fear.

Since we no longer teach our children how to face their own terror, they are plagued by that terror throughout their lives. They are terrified of failing in a myriad of ways that flow unconsciously (and often consciously) into their adulthood. They often try to avoid their inner terror by piling up accomplishments and credentials, by accumulating material wealth, or by various types of addictions. But no matter how much they pile on, they cannot really bury their terror. Failing outright or getting out of the race doesn't work either, because these two approaches hold their own terrors.

Once I knew a man who was failing at everything. His business went bankrupt, and his marriage ended in divorce. His therapist at the time told him that he had never known a man who needed to fail as much as my friend did. At the time, my friend thought his therapist was crazy, but he was right. My friend needed to fail in order to face his own terror, because if he didn't face it, he would never become an authentic person. After all, his earlier success at marriage and in business had been at least half motivated by unconscious terror and he had been *very* successful. His failing life drove him into therapy, and there he had a chance to carefully reflect on the story of his life. His fear of appearing a failure had driven him to create the picture of success. But he had never been able to stop long enough to question whether all he was doing had any real meaning or fulfillment for him.

Since this experience, I have worked with a number of successful men in many different professions who felt that they weren't living authentically, but were unable to face their deep-seated fears.

Vampires were common in their dreams, symbolizing both their terror and the murderous nature of their situations—situations that fed on their vitality. Often, this terror drove them further and further into their careers and out of life.

Until a man can face his terror and risk having his view of himself—his public face—burned away, he remains a ghost devoid of heart and vitality. Only after a man can face his terror, especially the terror of failing, can he begin to become fully human, fully alive, passionate, and compassionate. Primitives seemed to know this fact instinctively, which is why initiation rites began with terror and evolved into ordeals. After surviving these initial steps, the boy-man was ready for the teachings of manhood, sexuality, the lore and history of the tribe, and spirituality.

But men need another kind of courage in order to face the reality of adult life. This is the courage of EROS, the archetypal principle of relatedness. The courage of EROS often requires a man to lay down his defenses and stand open to suffering, to sacrifice for other things that are important to him. On different levels—courtship, family, fatherhood, community, and during responsible old age—men must nourish the development and maturation of EROS. Odysseus had to fulfill this virtue to become a mature king, journeying inland to finally plant his oar in the ground where no one would recognize it. By performing this act, he gave up his adventurer-warrior life to take up his responsibility as king of the realm and husband to the queen.

You may recognize that this same theme is repeated in the Grail legend, which is much closer to our time. The legend represents the quest for the Holy Grail, the spiritual container of life's vitality. This quest is the culmination of the reign of King Arthur. In it, the Fisher King has been wounded in adolescence and as he has grown older, his entire land has become a wasteland. It can only be renewed by the Grail. Deeply impressed by a series of spiritual signs, King Arthur sent his knights to search for the Grail shortly after the Feast of Pentecost. Sir Percivale was the knight who had the healing vision of the Grail and married the Grail Maiden. In this story, both healing and reconciliation are brought about and the masculine and feminine are united. Sir Percivale, like Telemachus, had an absent father and had to venture into the world of knighthood to discover and develop himself.

Nourishing Life: Spirituality and Instruction

The wisdom stories of the old societies connected them to the great questions of life: Why am I here? What is the purpose of life? What is our place in the universe? How do I live? The stories were passed on by the old ones, the grandfathers and the grandmothers, thereby relating both storyteller and listeners to the ancestral spirits of their people. For centuries, it was the job of the Fathers to shepherd the culture and pass on the spiritual traditions that could inform the development of boys into young men and guide them into their approach to life. In this process, the young men learned to sanctify life as their society understood it, thereby making life into a holy task.

As our society developed, a curious thing happened to this process. Our recent ancestors came from a variety of spiritual traditions. The men who arrived in the new world had to take up the challenge of making a new country along fresh political and economic lines. This challenge forced them to concentrate on the externals of life, allowing spirituality, by default, to fall into the world of women. This is not to criticize women but to point out that men deserted part of their traditional responsibility and unconsciously allowed an impossible burden to fall on women and institutions.

To make matters worse, this transition occurred without allowing women to "feminize" the form and structure of the spirituality for which they became responsible. In other words, women could not be authentic; they could not be their true selves in this new responsibility. Their task was to support the skeleton of spiritual values even while the flesh was withering—and to do so without the opportunity to add their own life to the sick patient. In loose terms, the practical, social values of Tom Sawyer's Aunt Polly rushed to fill the gap where the influence of the father was missing.

The loss of masculine spiritual responsibility seemed apparent to me as a boy in the fifties. I remember many occasions when my own or my friends' mothers tried to instill spiritual values by nagging their husbands and children to attend church. Our fathers couldn't communicate spiritual consciousness to us because they had lost it themselves. I don't know a single case in my generation where someone's father or school counselors encouraged them to become a dreamer, a poet, or a mystic.

Yet these attributes have been great masculine qualities since the dawn of time. Every great warrior culture from the Celts to the Samurai incorporated these qualities. Throughout history, the highest accomplishments of the human soul have come from aesthetics, poetry, and mysticism. Great myths such as *The Odyssey* teach us that the growth of the spirit depends upon the depth to which it has descended into the darkness of itself. It is in the underworld that the blind seer, Tieresias, reveals the pattern Odysseus must follow. And it is only after this experience that the shade of his mother instructs him to return to the "light." But our fathers had evolved into a drive for pragmatism, material success, security (a result of the depression), and conformity in a concrete outer world buried in increasingly abstract and worn out old forms of spiritual values.

When fathers failed in their spiritual responsibilities, what filled the hole in their children's personalities? To a large extent, it was the masculine side of women—their negative animus in Jungian terms (there is a positive side as well). This event happened not only because men had abdicated their spiritual responsibility but also because they abdicated their presence. Men were seldom there in the home or in schools during children's formative years. The negative animus of our culture concretized spirituality into the concrete rules of "good" behavior that may seem to be generally true, but do not give meaning and expression to an individual life. (A friend of mine once told me that he and his dad had the same father, his grandmother's animus.)

Joseph Campbell noted the results of this evolution as early as 1946 in *The Hero With a Thousand Faces.*

We remain fixated to the unexorcised images of our infancy, hence disinclined to the necessary passages of adulthood. In the United States there is even a pathos of inverted emphasis: the goal is not to grow old, but to remain young; not to mature away from Mother, but to cleave to her. And so, while husbands are worshipping at their boyhood shrines, being the lawyers, merchants or masterminds their parents wanted them to be, their wives even after 14 years of marriage and

two fine children produced and raised are still on
the search for love... .[8]

Our institutions, even the secular institutions such as schools, perform a covert type of spiritual formation. Their hidden curriculums of competition and grades (versus truth or knowledge) and non-participatory learning probably shape the character of our children more than the subjects they study. Churches, television, marketing institutions–just about everyone chips in to the covert spiritual instruction of our children when we have abandoned the task.

Perhaps we are now in a spiritual mid-life crisis in our society. In individuals, such crises are preceded by a sense of failure and loss that deepens into the crisis itself. But as with individual ones, if we face the cultural crisis directly and consciously, we will eventually develop a clearer sense of ourselves and a more mature culture. For better or worse, the old ways, the building blocks of our cultural foundations are behind us. But as the old alchemists did, we can dig up our own "prima materia" and work toward our own transformation.

It may not be easy, since spirit and spirituality are difficult things to discuss. Jung considered spirit in the following ways:

> *Those sayings or ideals that store up the richest experience of life and the deepest reflection constitute what we call 'spirit' in the best sense of the word. When a ruling principle of this kind attains absolute mastery, we speak of the life lived under its guidance as 'ruled by the spirit,' or as a 'spiritual life.'*
>
> *...Anyone who is conscious of his guiding principle knows with what indisputable authority it rules his life. But generally, consciousness is too preoccupied with the attainment of some beckoning goal to consider the nature of the spirit that determines its course.[9]*

In primitive cultures and civilizations, it was the vision of the

master, the shepherd, and the *Fathers* who personified the guiding
principles of life and the society. Often images of these guiding
visionaries became symbolized and represented by elders, priests,
kings, and prophets.

Jung continues his discussion:

> *I believe, therefore, that a spirit which accords
> with our highest ideals will find its limits set by
> life. It is certainly necessary for life, since a mere
> ego-life, as we well know, is a most inadequate
> and unsatisfactory thing. Only a life lived in a
> certain spirit is worth living. It is a remarkable
> fact that a life lived entirely from the ego is dull
> not only for the person himself but for all concerned.
> The fullness of life requires more than just an ego;
> it needs spirit, that is, an independent, overruling
> complex, for it seems that this alone is capable of
> giving vital expression to those psychic
> potentialities that lie beyond the reach of ego-
> consciousness.*

> *But, just as there is a passion that strives for blind
> unrestricted life, so there is a passion that would
> like to sacrifice all life to the spirit because of its
> superior creative power. This passion turns the
> spirit into a malignant growth that senselessly
> destroys human life.*

> *Life is a touchstone for the truth of the spirit. Spirit
> that drags a man away from life, seeking fulfillment
> only in itself, is a false spirit—though the man too
> is to blame, since he can choose whether he will
> give himself up to this spirit or not.*

> *Life and spirit are two powers or necessities
> between which man is placed. Spirit gives meaning
> to his life, and the possibility of its greatest
> development. But life is essential to spirit, since its
> truth is nothing if it cannot live.*[10]

It is worth repeating that spirituality has meaning only when it is lived out in everyday life. This is why the transformative Christian story (which we stubbornly refuse to understand) has such a powerful psychological message—Christ as spirit incarnated in matter. In our struggle for spirituality, the struggle our fathers never talked about except for an occasional platitude, we often find ourselves trying to transcend life, as is often the case in new age spirituality. If we follow this tendency, we can become so idealistic that we cannot possibly live up to our own ideals. We constantly feel like failures, which leads to a host of other problems such as fundamentalism, charismatic movements, gurus, despair, avoidance, cynicism, and so on. All of these problems represent a failure to embody spirituality in our living experience. Unembodied spirituality is not a failure of our religious institutions. They have *no* life of their own separate from the life with which we endow them. No, unembodied spirituality is a failure of the Fathers and Grandfathers.

We must follow the thread of spirituality backwards for a while in order to regain the part spirituality plays (or does not play) in our modern lives. Many great modern psychologists have told us that we are, in Irving Yalom's phrase, meaning seeking creatures. Yalom goes on to say that:

> *Biologically, our nervous systems are organized in such a way that the brain automatically clusters incoming stimuli into configurations. Meaning also provides a sense of mastery: feeling helpless and confused in the face of random, unpatterned events, we seek to order them and, in so doing, gain a sense of control over them. Even more important, meaning gives birth to values and, hence, to a code of behavior: thus the answer to* why *questions (Why do I live?) supplies an answer to* how *questions (How do I live?).* [11]

If we extrapolate a bit we can further say that we are cosmos-seeking creatures. An evolving culture requires an evolving cosmology. The key insight of depth psychology is the consciousness we create is the foundation of our psycho-spiritual cosmos. So, as we follow the cycle of transformation, we always end up back at the beginning but on a different level and with a renewed sense of purpose about our lives. Then we must take up the challenge of how to inform our sons and our daughters of these values.

Young people are hungry for adventures of the soul. We fathers need to get back into a passionate engagement with the great issues of life and reunite our young people with them. We need to inspire them by who we are and what we do rather than leave their inspiration to the media and the market place. And this means, of course, that we must be with them and they must know us. If we do, then perhaps we can guide the rebellious instinct of adolescence away from sour withdrawal, drugs, depression, and cynical nihilism—and toward a life that is more vital, courageous, and creative. When in touch with a guiding spirit, youth wants to make a contribution to LIFE, where their lives become an expression of themselves and not a sacrifice to their rebellion and their ancestors' failures.

Getting in touch with our lost spirituality will take courage. Joseph Campbell urged people to follow their bliss, and a lot of people have tried. Unfortunately, too many of them missed or quickly forgot what he said about focus and commitment.

> *Stay with it, no matter what people tell you... Can you endure ten years of disappointment with nobody responding to you, or are you thinking that you are going to write a bestseller the first crack? If you have the guts to stay with the thing you really want, no matter what happens, well, go ahead.* [12]

Uninitiated men pursue a shallow form of bliss because they want to be happy and expect the world to give them exactly what they want. Too many are still mother's boys lacking both the courage and the spirit to open the possibilities of life.

Our institutional Fathers and many well-intentioned real fathers told us to choose careers that are practical, that have money in them, that present a sure route to success. Now, as we try to break out of this choice, the same father (either real or as an inner part of our psyche) starts to ask: "What about your future? What about your retirement plan, your health insurance? What about your responsibilities, your spouse, your children, your home?" If we really want to live an authentic life, a life we can pass on to our children, we must have the courage to violate someone else's cultural "shoulds."

We need more than courage to discover the spiritual values of adults. We also need the wise old ones—the ritual elders and grandparents—to balance the severity, practicality, and ambitions of our personal and cultural parents. The wise old ones have perspective on life. They believe in the desire and power of youth. They understand that even if youthful pursuits lead to suffering, these pursuits also can lead to a truer experience of living and, through suffering, can lead to wisdom. They remind us that the function of society in this country is to cultivate the individual, and that the function of the individual is not to support the society except under this perspective. Where do we find our spiritual instructors, our wise old men, our "Grandfathers," our spiritual warriors, and our holy fools (who can constantly reconnect us to the spontaneous, creative imagination of the clown and child within each of us)? They are all around if we stop and look for them, in our present as well as our past.

When George Washington surrendered his seat of power and returned to being citizen Washington, George III was said to have commented that "This will be the greatest man of the century." C.G. Jung experienced his most productive years after the age of sixty, when he was seized by his daimon to struggle with the issues of the soul within himself, culture, and humankind. He was not a peaceful old saint. Martin Luther King Jr. expressed the dream that we should all be judged by our character and not the color of our skin. How often do we hear the word "character" anymore? In *She Wore A Yellow Ribbon,* John Wayne's wonderful movie about masculine development (which was unjustly ignored after he became a negative cliché), he plays an old army officer who, in the final minutes of his service, sits down with the old Indian Chief and says it was the job of *old men to prevent wars.* And then he goes on to do so using the skill of a lifetime and positive aggression—without a lot of bloodshed.

In Jungian psychology it is the analyst's function to bring an individual's consciousness and unconscious together in order to arrive at a new attitude toward life. In a similar way, if we cannot find the things we need in the outer world, we must go into our own unconscious depths to find them. If the initiating elders and the spiritual Fathers and Grandparents in the real world do not inspire us, we must dig into ourselves, our legends, our myths, fairy tales, dreams, history, and traditions in order to find their images. Then we must put these eternal images and ancient traditions in touch with the fragmentation and dissolution of the present in order to gain a new understanding of ourselves and our society.

Earlier, I mentioned that in the process of developing modern American society we had dealt a severe psychological wound to the feminine in our culture. As we wounded the feminine, we also impaired our society's mothering capacity and as a result several generations have grown up without a basic affirmation of themselves and without a sense of trust in life and in the world. Now we have just finished discussing the basic FATHER wound of our time—the inability to give meaning and direction to our lives, the spiritual wound. These wounds show us the depth of our problems—these wounds have hit us in the very foundation of our personal and collective development.

A Note for Women

In the last two sections I have focused more on the initiation rites for men than the ones for women which may lead you to wonder if this book should really be read by women. Please keep in mind, first, that my own experience is with masculine initiation and, second, that the Fathers had very little to do with feminine initiation rites in primitive societies. The feminine rites were women's mysteries just as the masculine rites were men's mysteries.

In some Native American tribes, though, there was a notable exception to the above rule. In these cases, the young woman was given instruction by a shaman, often a man. We could speculate that he may have been considered androgynous or was there to show that masculine nature can also be healing, supportive, and spiritual, but I think his masculinity was significant for two reasons.

First, the woman's father is the first male figure who makes a significant impression, perhaps the founding impression, on her own masculine personality component. The intervention of the shaman in a girl's initiation helps her internalize the spiritual authority of the Fathers by separating her from her literal father, as the initiators help the man separate from his mother by kidnapping him.

Secondly, the masculine component in a woman's personality has to go through a psychological maturation process similar to the maturation process experienced by men in their initiation ceremonies, such as the development of courage, self-discipline, and spiritual instruction. At some level we are always talking about ourselves as total human beings whether we are discussing the development of men or women.

Sexuality: The Abandonment of the Sacred

The history and lore of primitive societies contained the sacred traditions and symbols that supported that society's spiritual principles. Experiences with nature, including human nature, that inspired either awe or dread usually were symbolized in sacred form. Thunder indicated the presence of a powerful god. The fertility of nature was so important that human sacrifices were often made to nature gods, and a ritual path outlined the journey of life. This sacred symbolism helped channel the numinosity of these experiences, their radiant or ominous power, and allowed people to relate to them in a less dangerous and overwhelming manner. And one common experience that has carried numerous symbolic meanings throughout the centuries—from the fertility of the earth to the creation of the cosmos—is the union of man and woman.

Even today, we often find that the most emotionally charged memories of our lives cluster around the cosmic dance of eros. The first date, the first kiss, the prom, the first sexual experience, marriage, the birth of a child, all of these still carry numinous qualities. The darker side of sexuality—being caught playing doctor by critical parents, being shamed for exploring, sexual abuse, rape, or the betrayal of infidelity—can still cast a shadow on our personalities that may last for years.

While sexual love is rarely the solution to any problem, I can say as an analyst that sexuality is one of the greatest helps to the individuation process. The sheer pain, terror, and glory of it often provide my patients with the motivation for analysis, the courage to grow, and the faith (or desperation) to take risks. Sexuality is often the crucible of transformation. Jung commented:

> *One often hears the question: why should the erotic conflict be the cause of the neurosis rather*

than any other conflict? To this we can only answer: no one asserts that it must be so, but in point of fact it frequently is so. In spite of all indignant protestations to the contrary, the fact remains that love, its problems and its conflicts, is of fundamental importance in human life and, as careful inquiry consistently shows, is of far greater significance than the individual suspects. [13]

Anyone who doubts this significance need only look through the last twenty years of popular women's magazines and see which topic occurs most often.

When the primitives were instructed in sexuality, the instruction was done, as usual, by the wise old ones, the shamans or ritual elders. The symbols and forms of sexuality were thus endowed with reverence. This endowment was no accident. Eros was recognized as a biological urge that transcended human control while at the same time binding, protecting, and renewing the species. As a result, sexuality was sacred, both radiant and ominous. As a corollary, both marriage and childbirth also were considered sacred–their own spiritual forms.

Where marriage was not a matter of politics or barter, the young man often had to earn his bride. He had to demonstrate that he could take on the responsibilities of a family and prove that he was worthy to become one member of a twofold being. Frequently, sexual intercourse was then a sacrament celebrating the marriage, symbolically uniting the two and through the inner nature of desire bringing forth the immortal image of creativity.

In terms of our inner journey, the images of this process symbolize finding the source of our own life, our energy, and our capacity for revitalization. In *The Odyssey* the temptress Circe shows us what happens when the symbolism of this sacred process becomes profane. Sex without love and a symbolic container turns us into pigs. When we allow our instincts to lose their religious significance, we become their indulgent servants, imprisoned by our own wants. In this state we become the unsuspecting victims of our natures, bringing out the animal side in each other. Hermes, the god of boundaries and travel, and the connecting guide to the underworld as well, instructed Odysseus in his approach to this problem. He was to carry a plant (nature) representing balance (black and white) and use his masculine strength and discrimination (his sword) as he approached Circe—but he was to do her no violence. We must not be violent in this area because at a deep level it is the sacred ground of our renewal. After this confrontation, Circe was transformed from a danger into a helpful guide in Odysseus' journey toward his higher self.

It is the *spirit* of these sacred forms that connects the forms to life. When we reduce sexuality and reproduction to mere social conventions, we lose their spirit and mystery. As a result, we end up with rules to either obey or disobey—the famous "shoulds" and "oughts" of pop-psychology—that offer little living relationship with life. Once again, Fathers took the easy way out and abandoned their responsibility to teach, guide, and inform to marketing, religious, and educational *institutions*. When we institutionalize sexuality and reproduction, we lose not only their spiritual dimension but also the human numinosity that gave birth to them. Our humanity decreases when we reduce the sacred to the profane. When we do this, the numinosity of this fundamental life force is driven into our unconscious and will backfire into our collective lives in destructive ways as it has now done. In spite of our advanced technology, modern medicine, and sex education, our society continues to suffer from sexually transmitted diseases, unwanted pregnancies, fatherless children, younger girls becoming pregnant, drug addicted and deformed babies, and a general malaise in almost every area having to do with sexuality.

Somehow we have managed to secularize sexuality and reproduction, practically reducing them to entertainment and lifestyle, and at the same time we've become culturally obsessed with intimacy and relationships. This split between heart and mind, body and spirit, does not set us free. Instead it leaves us unbalanced and plunges us eventually into pain and chaos, as we can see all around us on every level of society. I'm not advocating a return to the old ethics that functioned on shame and guilt (although shame and guilt have their legitimate function). Healing comes by struggling to bring more consciousness to life, not by regressing.

A large number of men and women are trying to restore

stability in this area. Many of them have turned to periods of celibacy in the midst of their sexual pain and confusion. They aren't trying to achieve some type of spiritual transcendence over their body. But by holding their sexuality within (not suppressing or repressing it), they can both acknowledge its sacred dimension and claim this sacredness for themselves. By separating their sexuality from the cultural norms and suffering the tension of this sacrifice, they can take a passionate look inward. Celibacy helps them clarify their personal values, and this clarity lets them make more authentic personal choices.

Mircea Eliade[14] considered the sacred as part of the structure of consciousness so as the social forms of the sanctity of sexuality decay, it becomes our *individual* task to restore the sanctity of sexuality to our own lives.

Fathers must reclaim their sense of joy and exuberance in the development of their adolescents as well as their ability to encounter, inform, and inspire them in the realm of human relationships. And in so doing, they can return the sacred to society.

4

Past, Present, and Future: Life's Perspective

> *... the present flows out of the past, and the future will flow out of it. So for the fullness of the present one must not forget the past and the future. One has no understanding of the present if one has no knowledge of the past and of the future.*

> —M. L. von Franz

Most of us simply want to grow up and get it over with. The problem is that few of us, old or young, have any idea of what "grown-up" means except in the vaguest terms. If the so-called *grown-ups* don't know what grown-up means, how can we instruct the young in self-responsible adulthood and how can they know when they have achieved this level of maturity? If our experience of adulthood is so ill focused that Joseph Campbell could insist we are still worshipping at our childhood shrines, is it any wonder that our children and our culture are so confused? And this situation becomes even more confusing if we try to tackle the notion that "maturing" goes on as long as we live.

Primitive life was harsh, with constant threats from disease, starvation, and wild animals. While modern life has tamed most of these threats, it also has introduced a host of new ones. Whether in wars, revolutions, suburban or urban wilds, we need more than ever the training for survival. The roots of our survival are more psychological and spiritual than we realize, and we still need the lessons of the old initiation rites. Though these rites appeared severe, they remind us of the realities of life and that we must develop strength, independence, and spiritual self-reliance. If we rely too much on society to care for us, we take comfort in an illusion that thwarts the spirit of life.

Primitives and their mythologies focused on the meaning of the individual in the group. The initiates learned to take their place in the tribe, the "chosen people" or the "human-beings." Those who were foreign or in some way alienated from the group did not fully exist. In most tribes, the community replaced the parents in the initiate's personal psychology.

Now the emphasis has been reversed. Throughout America's short history, there has been a potent American dream that goes beyond the invention of products and improvements in the standard of living. It involves the invention of *self* and the establishment of a society that protects and enhances the individual. Even though we often forget this dream ourselves and slide into the shallow trough of individualism, this dream continues to inspire the twentieth century world.

Joseph Campbell noted this recent reversal:

> *The hero-deed to be wrought is not today what it was in the century of Galileo. Where then there was darkness, now there is light; but also, where light was, there now is darkness. The modern hero-deed must be that of questing to bring to light again the lost Atlantis of the co-ordinated soul.*[1]

Modern western culture has also generally associated the notion of mind, spirit, or soul with the idea of the FATHER or the masculine principle and body or matter with the MOTHER or the feminine principle. Jung tried to bring some balance to these notions by referring to the soul as feminine and proposing that all of us include both masculine and feminine psychological components. Another of our healing tasks is to be able to consciously embrace both dimensions in order to evolve toward a unified wholeness, a state many non-Western mythologies already illustrate.

We also face the task of discovering our own position as fathers in the context of the modern world. We must be able to reach back into the past to see what the general patterns for former personal and cultural fathers have been. Then we can combine these patterns with our psychological knowledge in order to integrate them into our lives. That is, we must attempt to do consciously and individually what was once done unconsciously and collectively. The job sounds overwhelming, and it can be if we try to do it all at once. Fortunately, fatherhood is not a problem to be solved but a process of transformation to be lived.

The era of Homer and *The Odyssey* represented the period in history when the individual psychological journey was replacing the ritual pathways that had guided the primitives in earlier unconscious times. As our psychological development transformed, so did our relationship to our community. The dynamic relationship and tension between the individual and society was born. As we have progressed, we have reached a point where personal development and societal development are interdependent. It is only when we have come to terms with ourselves that we can have satisfactory relationships with others and our society. But we also need social interactions and relationships to come to terms with ourselves. Along these same lines, the responsibilities of fatherhood shifted from the tribal men's group carrying out the initiatory rituals to the individual father, a shift that has left us increasingly alone.

One result of this transformation is that modern fathers do not have to have all of the "answers"–though many fathers haven't realized this fact yet. The worst thing that parents can do is to train their children in religious creeds that they themselves either don't incorporate into their lives or incorporate rigidly without question. The best that many of us can do is to show our children our own struggle for spiritual self-knowledge. If we are intensely involved in this struggle, then our adolescents can deal with our ambiguities. In fact, if our spiritual search is a vital part of our lives, our adolescents will leave their encounters with us with a sense of hope and purpose that will let them forge values of their own. If our spiritual curiosity seems dead–if, for example, we don't give it our time; primitive men spent up to one-third of their time in spiritual activities–then our adolescents lose their respect for us as well as hope for themselves and our culture. We both need the vitality and inspiration of the constant struggle to infuse life with purpose and meaning. Rigid answers dry up life while an awareness of the struggles can inspire it.

The struggle to become a whole person begins when we examine the positions we were born into and try to understand objectively the people our parents were and how they influenced us—the conventions of our parents that we have internalized. We must find out who we are, how we carry forward their influence, and how our personal and cultural circumstances have shaped us. In addition, we must separate ourselves from the collective consciousness and the prevailing cultural attitudes of our time—the conventions of our societal parents or institutions.[2] Finally, we must actively seek our own place in the human drama.

None of this is easy, of course. Our view of what life ought to be seldom corresponds to what life really is, and as we struggle through the above process, we have to continually challenge assumptions that run so deep we may not have realized they were assumptions— things we have taken as given all of our lives. In the end, though, this process frees us from the old influences, the old images, and lets us build truer relationships with our parents, with others, and with the community in which we live. Other people lose their symbolic power—once powerful parents become little old men and women, bankers become ordinary folks trying to make a living, priests and professors become simple human beings. In short, *authority* figures take their proper place in our perspective.

The Cycle of Life

Father/son, mother/daughter, father/daughter, mother/son all live within our own nature. Not only the images of our real parents, but also the images from our genetic memories, the psychic history of past eras, the archetypal images are alive in us and will match their life cycle with our own. Metaphorically, there are pairs of ancestors doubling and redoubling back down the generations until the whole race of humankind flows into and out of the birth of each child.

Youth grows into age, psychologically as well as physically. But in addition, age transforms into youth, through its progeny, the creative fruit of life. Generally, in the first half of life, our vital energy flows into developing our sense of identity in the external world. At the midpoint of our psychological life, our energy changes direction like the tide and flows toward the inner realm, toward developing our place in the cosmic human drama. For fathers, these two halves of life intersect. As our tide is turning, our children usually are becoming adolescents and entering the great struggle of identity development. The images of this psychological intersection are symbolized in mythology in the parallel journeys of transformation illustrated in the stories of Telemachus and Odysseus.

Often, this intersection shows up in our lives as a rift between a father and son or daughter. This rift could become a source of creative energy if it is embraced and transformed, but the union of these two psychic states is no simple handshake. The procedure requires trials, usually by emotional fire (anger and conflict), the willingness to keep trying to encounter each other, despite the conflict.

Within each of our personalities, this eternal mythical theme of the green youth confronting the sinister old man symbolizes an inner conflict between the formless potential of youth—unlimited possibilities still closely related to the MOTHER—and the concrete facts surrounding a specific life—the hard reality contained in the FATHER. To each, the other side initially appears as death. To the youth, the old man, often symbolized by the father, seems devoid of life, spontaneity, and emotions. He seems to be the institutionalized ego standing for law and order, and since many real fathers have become petrified in their conscious, materialistic systems and structures, their children often act out, disregarding laws and personal safety, becoming depressed, anorexic, or involved in other expressions of injured youth.

A good bit has been written about devouring or abusive fathers. In mythology Cronos or Saturn devours his children. Zeus and Oedipus slay their fathers. But less has been written on the opportunity the conflict between fathers and sons can provide. Growth requires symbolic deaths that are seldom easy. For adolescents to develop into adults, they must make choices and commitments and suffer the corresponding death of possibilities. Parents who keep telling their children, "I only want you to be happy" or "You can do anything you want to" are not only not helping their children, they are infecting them with our cultural pathology of remaining fixated to childhood. Adulthood means narrowing the choices.

There is a substantial symbolic death for the father side of our personalities in this transaction, too. The father has to accept the

death of his own youth and understand that some absolute limita-
tion has become absolutely inevitable. This death includes the
acceptance of his own physical decline and the future certainty of
the death it was so easy to deny during youth. This reality demands
either a deepening spirituality, denial, or despair. No wonder we
fight so hard against it.

The conflict between youth and age brings us face to face
with another death as well. Individually and culturally, we
naturally resist the idea that our future consists of a series of often
painful deaths and births. We fight this truth. We try to establish
a system of ideals, virtues, goals, and advantages as we enter
adulthood and then try to stick with them no matter what. We
don't want life to be a process we can't control. We want to reach
a secure point of arrival. We want the answers and even in
analysis long to "get it right." Perhaps we need this goal-directed
orientation in order to handle the tasks of family and profession
in young and middle adulthood. But in the end we have to let this
perspective go and focus on a deeper orientation toward life.
Society doesn't support this change and often considers it
dangerous or irresponsible. In order to turn toward our inner
world and maturity, our own *world view* must die and be transformed.

Adolescence — The Gift of Renewal

Youth at its best carries energy, zeal, idealism, understanding, and freshness, just as adulthood at its best includes realism,
structure, experience, wisdom, and compassion. But when youth
is not at its best, as it often is not, it includes omnipotence,
excessive daring, an inability to face life and make choices, an
inability to ground a sense of destiny into practical reality, and
the risk of becoming lost in causes. This image of youth can
become stranded in *Never-Never Land–The Land of the Lost Boys*,
never maturing, always lost in romance and fantasies, alienated
from the FATHER. Such youths (mostly boys, but this applies to
a girl's animus as well) are always trying to prove something to
the woman, whether she is present or fantasized, and at the same
time always run away from her. A young girl likewise flees her
feminine nature. In Kierkegaard's terms, these youths try to be
themselves without ever choosing themselves.

When adulthood is not at its best, it lacks imagination and is overly authoritarian, melancholic, and unwilling to take risks. Such adults can turn the "light of knowledge," tradition, humor, discipline, a striving for excellence, and all of the great masculine values into deadly poisons for the soul. This situation was clearly illustrated in the movie *Dead Poet's Society*. In this movie, the institution of a private school with a *fine tradition* and the ultraconservative father of a boy who wanted to be an actor turned the attributes of the cultural Fathers into an emotional and psychological poison. The result of this combination was the suicide of the boy and the destruction of a truly creative teacher. Needless to say, the masculine sides of modern women can be as infected by this poison, emanating from their fathers, our institutions, and their mother's animus as men are.

"The boy gives birth to the man," so the old saying goes, and the daughter also gives birth to the woman. In a general sense, youth represents the energy of life. Mature adulthood provides the proper forms to guide, direct, and develop this energy. Jung notes:

> *Energy in itself is neither good or bad, but neutral, since everything depends on the* form *into which energy passes. Form gives energy its quality. On the other hand, mere form without energy is equally neutral. For the creation of real value, therefore, both energy and valuable form are needed. In neurosis, psychic energy is present, but undoubtedly it is there in an inferior and unserviceable form.*[2]

Values are the intersection where adolescents and adults cross paths and often cross swords. Our teenagers, more often than not, explode into our lives, and family harmony goes out the door. Filled with fire and spunk (if the combination of overbearing parents and schools have not already squashed their spirits), they live on the emotional edge, rebelling, arguing, testing the limits, and thereby defining themselves in the context of the family and the world. They polarize us, causing us to either become more rigid or pay closer attention to the values that underlie the limits and lifestyle we stand for. Painful as it may be, our adolescents may help us realize that some of our cherished principles are simply old skeletons or that some of our values have decayed in the rough and tumble of life and need to be re-embodied and revitalized.

Adolescents bring us face to face with *emotional* life in a manner that can turn our world upside down. James Hillman has commented on our current attitude toward emotions and our reluctance to face the intensity of life.

> *This refusal to meet the challenge of emotion, this* mauvaise foi *of consciousness is fundamental to our "age of anxiety." It is characteristic of—even instrumental in—what has been called "the contemporary failure of nerve." We do not face emotion in honesty and live it consciously. Instead* emotion hangs as a negative background shadowing our age with anxiety and erupting in violence... emotion is always to be valued more highly than the conscious system alone. *This tends to run counter to the mainstream of thinking about emotion in the psychology, philosophy, and therapy of today.*[3]

If we are not too entrenched in our world view or overly dedicated to harmonious family life, teenagers can bring a fire of conflict into our lives that can help us return to the ground of our own being and authenticity. Anyone who has raised several adolescents also can testify that the process calls for fresh courage with each one, since they are all individuals. Teenagers are nature's gift to adults, returning us to honest living if we let them. Our interaction with them prepares us for the inner quest, the spiritual journey of the second half of life. If we don't let them, if we fail in our own maturation process, our sons and daughters will likely become pathological, often demonically so, and often until we clear up our own problems.

Adolescents in a healthy situation ask the right questions about life. They force us to deal with the fact that there is no money back guarantee that we will find the answers as life goes on, discouraging as this fact may be. But we can't respond by finding a way to avoid the questions of life—we can't truly avoid them. We shouldn't want to. We now live almost three times as long as people who lived only a few centuries ago. If we refuse to face the tough questions in middle age, we will have to live with that refusal for a long time.

Adolescents quickly and intuitively grasp their father's predicament (their mother's too for that matter). If the father living a provisional life, is worn out, discouraged, and maybe even sorry he chose the career he did–or if he is rigid, running too fast in order to maintain the illusion he has constructed–then the son will know it. Indeed, the son may see the problem more clearly than the father. Many middle aged men are not happy with their lives but don't quite realize that something big is wrong. They may always be tired, irritable, prone to addictions to food, alcohol, or exercise. But they are too afraid to give themselves time to reflect, so they may never realize the depth of their unhappiness until it is too late.

If such dads are also too distant, too closed, and too accepting of the cultural party line to be open to the insight their own children could bring them, then the children are also at risk. They may act out in a few cases, sometimes enough to get Dad involved in therapy and self-reflection. Or they may become distant and end up "just like you, Dad" as in Harry Chapin's old song, "The Cat's in the Cradle."

We need to find the courage to break the form of our increasingly narrow grown up ideology. We must be able to admit that, while our children must learn from our wisdom, experience, and patience, we must in turn revitalize ourselves and learn from their idealism, newness, innocence, enthusiasm, and boundless energy. It is a tragedy that so many of our adolescents, particularly in minority groups, have turned so demonic in their behavior and satanistic in their spirituality. I attribute this fact directly to the failure of the Fathers and our inability as fathers to face our own renewal, grow past our own limits, and accept the gift of adolescence.

Values and Kingship

As we have evolved from tribal life to a society formed of individuals, we have had to develop new levels of consciousness, to constantly renew our search for Self and a unified personality. One striking archetypal image has dominated this search for centuries: the image of the *KING*. In earlier times, the images of

KING, PRIEST, and FATHER were intertwined and projected onto a real person who ruled by the sanction of God. The literal king embodied the archetype of ruling order in the collective unconscious. As these outer kings began to become obsolete and their kingdoms fragmented, we have had to try to clearly differentiate the archetype from the real figure and to integrate it into our own personalities.

Symbolically, the KING represents the developing self-control and self-responsibility resulting in mature conscious awareness. A weak KING, representing a weak personality, leaves us vulnerable to the dangers of our instinctual and darker selves. In addition, early literal kings incorporated other images such as the HERO, the PRIEST, and the WISE OLD MAN. The father became the individual representative of these images in the family as every man became "a king in his own castle."

If we don't try to reclaim these old images of HERO, PRIEST, and KING and revitalize them, they turn into destructive institutions in our outer world (as the school as well as the father's attitude did in *Dead Poet's Society*). Devoid of life, these institutions are governed by rigidity and weakness rather than challenge and creativity, and they mold the personalities of our children to their negative, impersonal values.

I wish to emphasize the word *try*. None of us are going to become whole, individuated, together or whatever in this lifetime, nor should we think we have to be in order to be good parents. The idea is to be on the path of individuation, as consciously engaged in life as possible. Remembering the word of Aeschylus:

> *[Zeus] setting us on the road*
> *Made this a valid law—*
> *"That men must learn by suffering."*
> *Drop by drop in sleep upon the heart*
> *Falls the laborious memory of pain,*
> *Against one's will comes wisdom;*
> *The grace of the gods is forced on us*
> *Throned inviolably.*[4]

In our inner worlds, the KING is still a powerful psychological symbol on several different levels. The KING represents our greatest consciousness and also symbolizes our true self. He stands for the inner principle of unity that both unifies our personalities and facilitates our relationship to the world. An inner symbol the KING acts as the focal point for the health and creativity of the psyche. In order to have a healthy realm, the KING (consciousness) must unite with the QUEEN (life) so that both have equal emphasis in every personality.

But our inner cycles also evolve, mature, and grow old just like the king often does in fairy tales. As our dominant attitudes wear out or become wounded and negative, the old stories of the demise and transformation of kings can inform our inner journey with the ancient wisdom of our race. In *The Odyssey* alone, seven different kings play parts in the story. When this story is combined with *The Iliad*, we can see many of their evolutions. In fact, the stories of some of these kings have become pillars of western literature.

When this inner figure is healthy, our personality is united and creative, allowing us to lead lives that are productive, just, and compassionate. Our inner king nurtures and controls life in the realm. The rule of the healthy king is established by the grace of God—psychologically we might say by the sanction of the Self—and by the will and support of the people. In this sense, the king is a principle of creative life and not a principle of power.

When the symbolic king gets old, rigid, selfish, and arrogant, he fails to honor the feminine principles of life and the unconscious and trouble begins. If he fails to accept that the realm—the inner realm of the FATHER and the outer realm of his family and the culture—must grow, then he runs the risk of becoming a tyrant. If this happens, a new king must take the throne, bringing new unity, new visions, and a new reign. This transition must take place at every new developmental stage of life and often in between if we are to grow into old age rather than deteriorate into it.

Joseph Campbell[5] wrote that "The hero of yesterday becomes the tyrant of tomorrow, unless he crucifies *himself today.*" This statement applies most strongly when the father's path intersects the path of the adolescent. It is at this point, his psychological mid-life point, that the father must begin to relinquish the power of his ego consciousness (not the strength of his character—he must still be able to empower the new generation) in order to transform his world view, revitalize his values, and reorient his psychic energy toward the center and the Self. Fathers often experience this transformation as a crucifixion,[6] but it is necessary both for their individuation and for the new generation's.

Growth throughout life has always been a spiritual issue for humanity. Primitive man, as I have mentioned, spent as much as one-third of his waking time in spiritual matters, and becoming a grandfather or an elder was an honored position. If we make the mistake of simply considering our lives as problems to be solved or stages to make it through, we rob ourselves of our own humanity and turn our children into fearful ghosts separated from their own instinctual and spiritual selves.

When we come to the crucial intersection with adolescents, either inner or outer, they evaluate us, father and the Fathers, not by our achievements but by our *ideals*. To them—to ourselves if we are conscious—our ideals are manifestations of our grasp of life. Our ideals, lived as values, inspire us in our personal behavior and give us a basis to effect social change. The state of our society as well as my clinical experience reflect the fact that in terms of ideals and values, the king in our psyche is distant, weak, and feeble.

The archetypal image of ADOLESCENCE returns us to the pain and glory of being human—of having life and potential and the angst that neither of them is unlimited. As fathers, we need to get to work on relating to ADOLESCENCE in our inner world as well as to its carriers in the outer world. As we help form our children, we must also re-form ourselves and thereby the world.

PART 2:

TOUCHSTONES

5

Marking the Territory: The Psychology of Fatherhood

The latest investigations show the predominating influence of the father's character in a family, often lasting for centuries.

—C. J. Jung

Since the beginning of our kind, the image of the mother cradling her infant has symbolized the state of inner harmony. The foundation of our psychological relationship to life rests on our personal experience of this metaphor as infants. We carry this experience, in Erikson's terms "trust versus mistrust," straight into adulthood. It is the job of the Fathers to provide the emotional safety for mothers and children that insures the development of this image of trust in life. As we grow, we can then internalize this image as a basis for our development and self-actualization. If we have developed a sense of trust in ourselves and life, we are much less vulnerable to becoming overly dependent on other people, outer objects and situations, such as spouses, institutions, and conventional values.

Today we live in a world where our children are scared. Our inner unity and security is split. We are all overinvolved in the demands of outer worlds at the expense of our inner lives. We are so alienated from our own natures that we have practically forgotten that they even exist. Mother and child, as a metaphor or a concrete reality, are not safe in our world. The Fathers have failed in their most elementary task.

For several generations now, the expectant father in our culture has been portrayed in the media as an awkward, bumbling figure who can do little but get in the way. In the last few decades, men have become more actively involved in the birth process, coaching their wives through labor, and being present at the birth. But even though the involved father is an improvement on the buffoon pacing in the waiting room, and even though maternal men can sometimes be helpful and may make better mothers than their wives—is it appropriate that fathers take on the role of mothering? Should fathers become nurturing duplicates of mothers?

Joseph Campbell, when speaking of males, began by discussing Jane Goodall's chimps.

> ... *males control an area some thirty miles in circumference, and they know where the bananas are. When the bananas are failing in one area, they know where to go for more. They also are defenders. They defend against invasion by other tribes. And just in the primary way, the function of the male in this society is to prepare and maintain a field within which the female can bring forth the future.*[1]

The child psychiatrist D. W. Winnicott[2] maintains that the appropriate role of the father is similar to the natural role of male chimps—to provide a "protective covering" for the mother so that she can turn her full attention to bearing and nurturing the baby. Early infancy, when the world of the family begins imprinting itself on the infant's psyche, is a critical time in our emotional development. And much of the infant's view of the world is filtered through the mother's body and the emotional attitudes her body reflects. A mother who is nervous, anxious, or resentful of the birth will lead her child to feel out of adjustment psychologically. This child will have a personality founded on a deep sense of anxiety and mistrust in the world. A mother who is sufficiently gentle, loving, and emotionally secure (Winnicott calls this the "good enough mother" in order to counteract the illusion that mothers must be perfect) will help her infant develop a basic sense of trust in life and in their place in the world. Winnicott maintains that it is the father's role to provide the mother with the peace she needs to be a "good enough mother."

Of course, this greatly oversimplifies the situation. Life is complex, and the mother-infant relationship can be disturbed for any number of reasons, early deaths, illnesses, separations, or deprivations due to a myriad of crises. Also declaring mothers responsible for the relationship's success or failure is much too easy an answer. My point is that fathers, and the cultural Fathers, play an important part in this primary relationship.

Even though we are not chimps, with a need to defend our territory from intruders, we still need to defend our family (and ourselves) from fear. From a psychological perspective, the wounding of the feminine in our culture has led many mothers to mistrust the world and men to a greater degree than ever before, and this mistrust has affected our children. Also, we live in a fearful society. The *Atlantic Monthly* recently ran a lead article entitled "Growing Up Scared" that showed how all of our children in every socioeconomic level live with fear every day. Furthermore, we have created an economic system that requires both parents to work in many cases, almost guaranteeing stress for young parents. Finally, as human beings, our primary sense of security often comes from caring, trust, and emotional closeness, and our sense of community and family is very strained. The threats to parenting are more complicated and serious than ever. It is the Father's responsibility to consciously face them in order to create a safe society and a protective covering "to bring forth the future."

Father and Mother

As a baby emerges from the period of complete dependence on the mother, it becomes conscious of the father not just as a familiar figure, but as a figure who is also different from the mother. The presence of this additional parent reduces stress for both the mother and the child and adds balance and stability to the family in a healthy situation.

As the children continue to grow, they get to know their fathers as individuals and so learn more about a real relationship that includes love and respect. For his part, the father should let his children see enough of his real self over the years to demystify himself so that his children can relate to him as a human being, not as a god or distant figurehead. If so, a father can open up a whole new perspective on life for his children. When he joins them in play or takes them out, he adds valuable new elements to their experience and helps them see the world through a new pair of eyes.

As the father begins to have an influence on his child, he activates an archetypal pattern whose nature is opposed to that of the mother's. In elemental terms, the FATHER represents doing and the MOTHER being. This FATHER archetype determines our relationship to society, to reason, to the spirit and the dynamism of nature. The actual father carries this archetypal image in the life of the child, just as the actual mother carries the archetypal image of the MOTHER. It's vitally important to distinguish between the archetypes and actual fathers and mothers when we talk about a father helping a child "separate from the mother." What we mean is that in order to become adults, we must separate from our own dependency needs represented by the archetypal image of the MOTHER. This separation from the MOTHER doesn't necessarily mean alienation from your real mother unless perhaps she refuses to participate in the process of psychological maturation. And even while a father is helping his son separate from the MOTHER, he must support the real mother emotionally during the period of separation.

Psychological growth involves separating the archetypal images from the real parents and integrating them into our own personalities. This procedure happens on three levels. First, we separate from our mothers, then from our fathers, and then the *world* or *cultural* parents–the guiding social conventions of our time that can entrap us in societal obligations. This process takes years and, if it goes reasonably well, it gives us the opportunity to have a genuine relationship with both our parents and our own children. If the process goes poorly, usually because the parents fight against it in some way, then all parties are likely to wind up angry and resentful, or else dependent on or alienated from one another.

Many of my analysands are haunted by the commandment, "Honor your father and mother." They end up racked with guilt and shame because they feel they should "honor" a parent who intimidated and brutalized them through their entire childhood. In reality, they hate their parents, but they torture themselves thinking they should be able to forgive their parents because they "did the best they could." (The fact is, if someone has abused you, it is simply healthier and more human to *hate* them.)

To honor your father and mother psychologically means to be conscious of the images they have left within our personalities and of the power those images have to shape our destinies. We must honor these images or be victimized by them. Once we have become an *individual* and have differentiated from our parents, these inner parental images become companions and bless us with their special energy.

As before, we can find an illustration of this process in the elder wisdom of mythology. In Book Sixteen of *The Odyssey*, Telemachus and his father, Odysseus, are reunited by Athene. A very poignant passage outlines the process that enabled Telemachus to remove the godly (archetypal) image of his father and reconcile with the human being previously hidden by this representation. When first revealed by Athene, Telemachus refuses to accept the identity of his father. He responds with fear that Odysseus is not his father, but some god deluding him to increase his pain and sufferings and beseeches him for mercy. Odysseus replied:

> *No god, why take me for a god? No, no. I am that father whom your boyhood lacked and suffered pain for lack of. I am he!*[3]

Once again Telemachus rejected this possibility, saying:

> *... Meddling spirits conceived this trick to twist the knife in me...*[4]

Odysseus then instructed him to bear the manhood he had earned and conduct himself like a prince. With this admonishment, Telemachus accepted Odysseus as his father and they embraced and wept.

> *... Telemachus began to weep. Salt tears rose from the wells of longing in both men, and cries burst from them as keen and fluttering as those of the*

great taloned hawk, whose nestlings farmers take
before they fly. So helplessly they cried, pouring
out tears, and might have gone on weeping until
sundown, ...[5]

In this beautiful poetry we can experience the deep yearning
for, and the intense joy of, being able to reconcile with the
humanity of a parent. The eternal truth in this scene reminds us
that Athene, the goddess of wisdom and courage, must mediate
this reconciliation. We also must note carefully Odysseus' example, for it is the responsibility of the *parent*, specifically the
father to take the initiative and insist upon giving up his larger-
than-life image as well as insisting on his son's bearing himself
with maturity.

Father As a Model

The father is a model for his son, and a partial model for his
daughter, of how to live and operate in the world. This doesn't
mean that the mother can't also model competence in the world,
but given her biological function, she can't model separateness
from herself. The father more naturally represents authority,
civilization, and movement into the world and as a result
boundaries, space, and time. Jung states that the father is he that
moves in the world, like the wind, the guide and creator of
thoughts and airy images. He is the creative wind-breath—the
spirit, pneuma, *atman*.[6]

In mythology, the father gods give birth to civilization and
the mother goddesses give birth to life and nature. In a rough
psychological sense, the mother image gives birth to the child's
nature and the father image gives birth to a child's culture.
Winnicott maintains that the child's experience of mothering
determines his or her self-image and world view. The father is
more associated with how the child fits into that world view, the
child's social character. This is why the Fathers in archaic
societies presided over the *second birth* of their sons, their birth as
self-responsible adults and community members. The Fathers
were the ones who provided the spiritual and cultural values,
traditions, and instruction that would guide their sons as members of the community. And although the two roles overlap in

practice and neither mother nor father ever functions alone, the two roles are largely distinct.

This is why one parent can never fully replace two. If the father is absent, abusive, or distant, his children are going to have a hard time getting around in the world and developing a life that reflects their inner values. I know because in the last decade I have met a frightening number of young people whose dads did the *right thing*–good private schools and good colleges, the bills all paid. But when these kids got out of college, they had no idea what to do next and few could even plan a budget or balance a checkbook. Clearly we need good-enough fathers to go with Winnicott's good-enough mothers, good-enough fathers who can provide identity, competence, and confidence as a young adult enters life.

The Father as a Persona Model for the Son

"Persona" is the psychological term that refers to the face or faces a person puts on to confront the world, a person's gender identity, age, social status, or profession. In other words, our persona contains the components of our social identity. Over our lifetime, we may wear many personas and, at any given moment, we may combine several of them.

Often people misunderstand this term and think it only refers to our job or profession. If you ask someone to define themselves to a stranger, they may say "Hi, I'm Dr. Jones and I'm an internist." This notion is oversimplified. We can easily see in *The Odyssey* that many of the major figures took on different appearances as they dealt with different situations. When Athene traveled to Ithaca, she went dressed as a magnificent warrior. Later she assumed the guise of Mentes and then Mentor. Odysseus appeared back in Ithaca as a beggar. We can see in these examples that our personas have several roles. They facilitate our interactions with other people in different situations while protecting our inner selves. In addition, our persona, if healthy in relationship to the rest of our personality, gives us an outer face that effectively expresses our true selves in these situations.

As part of our personality, the persona is both useful and dangerous. It is useful because it's through our persona that we relate to the world, how we interact with other people and with social institutions. It is our personas that we bring to work, to PTA meetings, to our bridge club, to church. Psychologists often refer to the persona as the "social archetype" since it involves the legitimate compromises we must make to live in a community.

But if our ego identifies with our persona–if we *become* our job or social role–then the persona can become very dangerous. We lose touch with our inner ground and live solely by the external structures and responses of society. This leaves us vulnerable to the demands and opinions of other people and usually drives us to become rigid and brittle. Deep within, we become lonely and paranoid because we have lost our inner authenticity. I have dealt with many businessmen who have identified with their personas successfully and energetically, often in compensation to some early wound. They usually end up, as Joseph Campbell put it, having "climbed to the top of the ladder only to find out it was against the wrong wall." When they begin to realize this, they start to develop a "hollow" feeling often followed by dreams of vampires as I mentioned earlier.

The father, by his very existence and by the way he lives, models the workings of the persona for his sons, for better or worse. If his expectations for his son don't match his behavior ("Do what I say, not what I do"), then his son is in trouble. The son looks to his father for a model of how to maintain his authenticity; so if the father isn't living up to his own ideals, then the son will never learn how to live up to them either.

Also, our father's approval, disapproval, pride, or anger is our first experience with the social demands that are placed upon us. If a father tells his son he's not worth a damn and never will be, the son may go for decades feeling he's a failure no matter how successful he may be. But if a father guides and encourages his son as he differentiates his personality, the son will learn to experience himself as a PERSON, a capable person, a person with promise. Depending on how our fathers interact with us, we may either submerge our personal identities in cultural norms, even identify with failure, or else find our true identity as adults.

Father and the Daughter's Animus

The father is an equally important model for his daughters. The father is the human figure who begins the development of his daughter's image of her own inner masculine side. He is the first image of "Not-I" and the first image of a *lover* in her life. Whether her animus turns into a beast that constantly belittles her or is a loving guide rests to a great extent on her experience of her father.

And as the daughter grows up, her relationship with her father continues to shape her emotional and psychological development. As the first male figure in her life, he affects not only how she relates to her own masculine side but how she relates to men in general. How he reacts to her femininity will change the way she grows into her womanhood just as his modeling affects the way his sons grow into manhood. His attitude toward the world, work, relationships, and competence will mold the attitudes of his daughters as well as those of his sons. The father provides a model of authority, responsibility, decision-making, and objectivity.

When we throw out the old patriarchal authority (which is really dominance and, therefore, a false authority), we need to replace it with a model of authority based on values and inner authenticity. Our sons and daughters both need to develop confidence in their own inner sense of personal authority.

Our culture is in great danger when fathers do not provide a model for this authority. I have already talked at length about how absent fathers dump the problem of differentiation onto the child. But what is the danger when the so-called "soft-male" gets into fathering? If the father gets so far into the nurturing role that he is another mother, then his sons will have difficulty establishing their masculine identity and function in society and his daughters will grow up one-sided. A father does not have to present a macho image or disdain nurturing, but he needs to have some conscious awareness of himself and his values as a man.

6

Face to Face — Toe to Toe: The Search for Identity

The strongest and most fateful factor was the relationship to the father...

—C. G. Jung

The search for identity is the theme of *The Odyssey*. The son searches for his identity as a man. The father searches for his true self as he travels into the second half of adult maturity. Both are reconciled in the end on several levels. Grandfather, father, and son link together the past, the present, and the future. The reconciliation of the king and queen represent the reunion of the masculine and feminine elements or the conscious and unconscious parts of our personalities. The metaphorical images in the myth are strong, dynamic, and impressive. But let's leave them for a while and look further into the practical interrelatedness that goes on between developing parents and children as they interact in an effort to differentiate each other.

In previous chapters, we saw how our early relationship to our mothers, more than any other relationship, forms the foundation of our personality and our view of life and ourselves. We also saw how we first learned to be a significant and meaningful partner in a human relationship when we began to relate to our fathers. We can only become individuals as we define ourselves against another person. Since our mother is the first and for a while the only person in our life, we begin by defining ourselves against her. But because we depend so heavily on our mothers, cannot move outward into self definition until we learn that we can rely on someone other than our mother. We need this intermediate step before we can believe we can manage without leaning on anyone. The father, of course, is the best choice. He is separate from both the child and the mother, yet is as reliable as the mother, only in a somewhat different way. The father opens up a new option so that we, as children, have some choice about our close relationships. Relationships become a matter of preference rather than necessity.

As we grow toward adolescence, our search for identity intensifies. More than ever we need to be recognized as a PERSON, not only by our father in contrast to our mother but also by our father as the carrier of the FATHER archetype and the cultural sanctions. As we develop, we need to make a difference to the people important to us.

When speakers and writers talk about the father-shaped hole in our personalities, they are talking about the hole that forms if our fathers are not fully present for us to react against. R. D. Laing puts it like this:

> *... the person experiences not the absence of the presence of the other, but the absence of his own presence as other for the other.*[1]

Simply put, we need to make a difference by both giving and receiving. Adolescents are searching for a sense of identity, and part of this sense is an understanding of what is needed and wanted from them. Also, being needed and being personally important to someone else leads an adolescent to feel trusted and respected. In short, they feel valuable. Psychologists call this intertwining of reciprocal giving and receiving dependence and independence "mutuality."

Many of today's fathers are excellent *givers*. But they do not understand mutuality enough to be *receivers*. They appear distant, unresponsive, or impervious to their children. Like the Wizard of Oz, all that's known about them is rumors and superstitions. And when we actually meet them, they seem larger than life, ominous, and far too busy to deal with our little problems. These Oz fathers can generate a deep sense of failure in children who never see the man behind the curtain, a failure that may lie buried under driven achievement, rebellion or despair, and addiction. Often these men's wives feel like failures too, unless they've resorted to divorce. Both wives and adolescents can despair when they begin to question their capacity to mean anything to anyone, including themselves.

A sixteen-year-old boy I had as a patient once wrote the following piece:

> *The wind blows cold on the face of a shadow, cutting away illusion from reality, silence prevails on the world of shadows, I live afraid of reality, yet afraid of insanity, constantly torn between heart and mind, for I write from a poet's heart, with a brain of circuits and wires, living on the edge of reality, crying silently for the crimes I see committed, but I lack a voice, for I am only a shadow—a lonely element in the greater scheme of life, walking alone never lighted by the sun, for I live the life of a shadow.*

By normal standards, this young man's father was not a bad guy. He paid his son's support, carried the boy's health insurance, spent two weeks a year and alternate holidays with him, and had signed on to pay his son's college costs. He also telephoned every couple of weeks to stay in touch and supplied a liberal amount of platitudes.

Yet his son feels nonexistent and doesn't know how or who to be. He told me that the shadow in the poem is a form that always fits expectations and can't find its own true structure. Clearly, the young man is missing his ability to connect to his true self, even though his ability to voice his predicament is lucid and poignant. The traditional symbol of the father—the light of the sun, logos, and consciousness—is also conspicuously absent.

We cannot encounter our children in any helpful way unless we are fully engaged in life ourselves. This doesn't mean we have to live perfectly balanced, together lives. But we must be vitally and personally engaged in our lives and relationships, open to reflection, open to conflict, and open to our mistakes.

Two things happen when we're engaged with life. First we grow. We grow as the results of the experiences we have if we are vitally engaged in life and seek to live fully and reflect sufficiently to understand the themes and meanings that our life stands for. Then our children grow because we can give them a presence that gives substance to their presence. Moreover, they are less likely to become unconsciously trapped in our shadow side, the substance within us that we deny.

When a man encounters young people, he must conduct himself with integrity in order to teach or inspire them. Adolescents are quick to spot hypocrisy or paternalistic authority and just as quick to respect true dignity, humor, and honesty. In other words, adolescents can spot character.

As both sons and daughters become old enough, the father must be willing at times to step back and take a moral stand. If the father has enough character, his stand will enable his children to form their own values and ideals. They may accept some of his values. They may need to clarify some values of their own by rejecting his, with the resulting conflict. If so, the father should hold his ground without insisting that he maintain his patriarchal dominance. This means that if his children happen to be right, he must be willing to admit it. Only if he is willing to lose to them, allowing them to be different from him, can they develop their own perspectives. If he is too rigid and impersonal in maintaining his position, he may only be forcing them into more and more serious forms of rebellion.

This conflict can be painful, but it also can be exciting as we watch our children become individuals. We must realize that growing up can be a painful process, and the more we try to smooth their path past a certain point with our "mature" thinking, the more we are actually denying them the chance to struggle and develop consciousness, their own personalities, and deep meaning in life.

Time after time, I have come to the startling realization that adolescents I've worked with have no idea what their parents' values are. They know they should score high on their SATs and try for a good college (often under parental mandate: "Do well or you're sunk"). They know a few general values such as it's wrong to murder, steal, or smoke dope. But it's hard not to question these values given the way adults behave and the messages from advertising, TV, and the movies.

Fathers often have values but many are afraid to ask the questions that would bring these values to light and lead to a deeper relationship to life. Fathers have experience in the world but don't know how to convey it to their children. The father's separation from the family has cut off communication between himself and his children, which eventually creates either an antagonistic relationship or a passive, withdrawn father (even if he is authoritarian). In effect, too many fathers have given up.

Fathers must fight to reconnect with their children—to explain their values and how these values relate to the way they live. Men's lives have faded so far from home that kids no longer can learn of their fathers' world through osmosis. Fathers have to consciously forge the connecting links between themselves, their worlds, and their children. Fathers need to communicate their values of work, family, and politics to their children. Fathers also need to present a model of living that makes these values explicit—values that can't be seen are worthless to the family.

One good place to begin is with a willingness to argue with other family members within an atmosphere of love. If you're divorced, stand face to face and toe to toe with your children and listen to their hurt and anger without becoming defensive or self-justified. Be able to argue politics and ethics, and be sure to *listen carefully* to their views and present your own in a thoughtful manner—not in the "I am the parent, I know best" tradition. Keep your mind as open as you want theirs to be, and be willing to learn from them. Adolescence is a time when everything changes, when our children first face the great questions of "Who am I?" "Where am I going?" and "What is the meaning of this world?" If we listen to them, we may run across some exciting and provocative insights. But don't be a blank screen. Stand up for your own values, even if it means the fight will go on. Even if your children don't agree, they will learn from your integrity. And be prepared in the end to let your children go, helping them develop their values as they leave.

Also, a father must intercede for his children's right to be who they are, good or bad, and stand with his children against the children's mom and the current cultural values if need be. Many fathers I've dealt with find this a fearful task, but what are we all so afraid of? Why are we afraid if our children don't take the SATs over and over, or go to a small state college, or don't go to college at all?

Why can't we have some faith that if we live our values openly and clearly and love our children, they will get the picture of life they need?

I appreciate the pressure of being a father, nowadays, feeling responsible for a family and having to go to work. And I don't mean to judge fathers past or present. But it is now time for we fathers to ground ourselves again in the important human values that have slipped away from us in the process of modern living. We need to reunite with the meaning, the joy, and the love that have faded more and more in the last few generations. Many of our fathers worked hard and selflessly for us—watching their own *bliss* slip away from them in the vortex of wars and changing economic and social patterns. We need to recapture our own *bliss*, both for our own sake and that of our children. Only by being people ourselves can we have the person-to-person encounter with our children that transforms our relationship from one of roles into one of humanness and, in the process, enables our children to find their own inner voice and authority.

Absent Father — Substitute Identity

During our century, the father/FATHER has faded into an institutional abstract, as you can see from Freud's concept of the super-ego and the institutional structures developed to improve our society. These institutions now dominate education, government, religion, and entertainment—all of the major areas in everyday life. As we entered into this century, men lost contact with their own natures. As a result, our greatest institutional achievements became founded on a one-sided, imbalanced lack of humanity. Paradoxically, our government depersonalizes the people it tries to help, our vast school system no longer knows its purpose, and our churches have little understanding of the nature and needs of the human soul.

The admirably civilized institutions we have created to employ, educate, and govern us often end up sapping our will to be self-responsible and adventuresome. Moreover, as Parker Palmer points out:

> *But if the problem with primitive knowledge was the overidentification of the knower with the known, our problem is the estrangement and*

alienation of the two. In our quest to free knowledge from the tangles of subjectivity, we have broken the knower loose from the web of life itself. The modern divorce of the knower and the known has led to the collapse of community and accountability between the knowing self and the known world.[2]

Palmer proceeds to say that our institutions give our children a covert type of spiritual education of their own, forming the personalities of our children as they formed us. The whole system of rewards and punishments in our schools and churches works to shape our views of ourselves and the world far more than any one-on-one personal spiritual teaching. We end up seeking a kind of knowledge that eliminates mystery and gives us control over every facet of life, even our religious faith. As a result, reality is always "outside" of us, and that is where we seek increasingly meaningless answers. Institutional, spiritual, and academic education does not try to locate and develop our sense of self in the world. It tries to get it out of the way.

The result is that our adolescents, like many of us, learn a slave ethic that bonds them to the *outer* world because there is no recognition of the inner world. They grow up to serve the social forms because without them life has no validity. At the center of their conscious personality lies a vacuum that comes from having no connection to the deeper Self or humanity. Adolescents in such an environment never learn how to question, how to learn in freedom, nor how to live in either free or committed ways (understand, there's a difference between being committed and being driven–anxiety is not passion). They never learn to be guided by an inner sense of truth. How can they possibly follow their *bliss*? A *shadow* can't even know what it is.

Of course these adolescents still have passions, but the institutions that shape their personalities drive these passions underground where their energy grows wild in the denied parts of ourselves–the shadow in Jungian terminology. This dark energy is what drives the growth of satanic cults and underlies the lyrics of heavy metal music. For instance, the rock group *Iron Maiden* recently sang:

The demon in your mind will rape you in your bed at night
The wisdom of ages, the lies and outrages concealed
Time it waits for no man
My future is revealed
Time it waits for no man
My fate is sealed

If I cancel tomorrow the undead will thank me today
Fly in the face of your prophets I mock your morality plays
The moon is red and bleeding
The sun is burned and black
The book of life is silent
No turning back

Only the good die young
All the evil seem to live forever[3]

A middle-aged man, Fritz Zorn, dying of throat cancer, felt his cancer was connected to the tears of his childhood and adolescence that had been choked back. The focus of his middle-class upbringing had been *appearances* based on material success and not passion. He expressed the above theme in even more personal terms.

> *I wanted to be "cast down into hell" so that I could be somewhere else, anywhere else than in that first thirty years of my life. And this is why I turned to the Satanic world to find salvation.*[4]

Directing and forming our passions so that they vitalize our life, art, and knowledge is a function of the Fathers and the personal father. The relationship between fathers and children is the foundation of soul-making. If we or our sons and daughters are spectators, no matter how practical and objective, we castrate the entire process of human development.

We need to revitalize and resubstantiate fatherhood in our culture. We need to recognize the value of the archetypal image of fatherhood, of ourselves as carriers of it, and our children's *need* to have it fulfilled. To be effective, a father and the Fathers must have a sense of importance and dignity. Until they do, the power of father love will remain entrapped in our psyches. Each of us must develop our awareness and father ourselves to start the process moving again.

Father Love — Nurturing, Destroying, Empowering

Earlier I noted that while the mother nurtures the child's emerging self-consciousness, the father stands as a guardian and protector of the mother-child field. Later, the father helps the child develop a sense of self by being a model of masculinity and a guide into the outer world of activity. It is within this process that father love finds its definition.

Mother love at its best fosters trust in life and holds, comforts, embraces, and protects us from the dangers that threaten us from the darkness of our inner nature. Father love supports the other side. It protects us from the dangers of the external world. At its best, it teaches, limits, directs, inspires, and empowers self-responsible development. To be whole, we need both types of love.

In our wounded, alienated world, we have become sentimental about nurturing and reduced it to a fairly primitive emotional experience connected to MOTHER. A good example of this trend is the recent interest regarding God as MOTHER. The idea certainly makes us conscious again of another aspect of God, and helps to balance an image that had become one-sided in a very patriarchal age. However, at a recent workshop I attended, a mass was performed using milk rather than wine. To me, this action showed that the meaning of father love and spirituality had been all but lost, and we run the risk of simply regressing to the other extreme of our former one-sidedness.

So while fathers may try to become more involved with nurturing their children, they must be careful not to use mothering as a model. Several legends and fairy tales tell how, when the mother is absent, the father may suckle his children, but he must slash his breast—and thus wound himself and his masculinity—to do so. If we lose sight of this fact, we lose sight of father love and the father's importance to the family and children. *Nurturing is not just nurturing*, and unless we are careful, we can give our children only half the love they need in the name of love.

Traditionally in western culture and religion, the mother's love for her children will always give them a second chance. The father's love, on the other hand, is always full of expectations. Forgiveness and atonement are always in relationship to the father. Rabbi Jacob Neusner[5] points out:

> *If God is only father there is no end to the hammer of justice.... If God Is only mother there is no end to the excess of our self-indulgence.*

A good psychological father wants his children to grow to become independent and self-responsible. He takes joy in their maturation. He encourages them, sets them risks they can handle and tasks that they can achieve, builds their confidence, empowers them. Such a father often communicates to his children a sense of quiet strength, steadiness, discipline, and sacrifice for causes greater than himself. When he is stern and commanding, it is out of Eros, out of love. He doesn't want to humiliate or shame his children or to engage their mother in a power struggle over them. He simply wants to free his children from the bondage of childish dependency and endow them with the spirit of life.

But father love often goes wrong. A father can't perform any of the above tasks if he is not there, either physically or emotionally. And often the father cannot accept the development and maturity of his children. He sets them important tasks, but often makes sure the tasks are out of their reach, or has so many criteria for success that his children cannot possibly succeed. The result is that his children are left with a feeling of failure and despair. They have to fail because their success would threaten his own spiritually failed position. His legacy to his children is a curse that robs them of their energy and the spirit of life.

When Odysseus was reunited with Telemachus, he accepted him and admonished him to bear himself with the adulthood he had earned. In Book Twenty-One, Odysseus faced a final test that enabled him to validate his identity, confirm his initiation into maturity, and win his bride and kingdom for the second time. This test consisted of stringing a bow that had formerly belonged to him, and then to shoot an arrow through the eyes of twelve ax heads in a row. As the bow was brought out, Telemachus took it and attempted three times to string it. On his fourth attempt, at which he probably would have been successful, Odysseus stopped him and he acquiesced. This gesture was a proper one for both of them because power and competition are no longer an issue between them. They were reconciled. Their relationship was healed and now one of adults. Neither needed to prove their power or question the power and identity of the other.

In the first part of this book, we described how the initiation process in primitive tribes helped the initiate internalize the psychological authority of his parents. The priestly or ritual father figures had the additional responsibility of initiating only a young man who had passed the tests, separated from childhood dependency, and demonstrated the courage to participate in life. Then the young man was considered ready to join the "twice-born," to become a father, a guide, and an initiator himself.

If the Fathers of our culture are indulgent and allow children to assume the roles of adult life when they aren't ready, chaos and tragedy result. We already have seen that the indulgent father who pays all the bills but offers no mutuality engenders a sense of failure and nonexistence in his children. The indulgent father who sets no tasks for his children dooms them to the fiery psychological death of Phaëthon as their spirit of life plunges back into the unconscious like a falling star.

We often think of the abusive father as the terrible destroyer symbolized by Cronos or Saturn. And so they are. Cronos (Saturn in the Roman tradition) is the archetypal image of the raging, devouring father. He was the son of Uranus (sky) and Gaia (earth). He castrated his own father to gain his independence. He then devoured all his own children except Zeus who had been hidden by his mother, Rhea. Cronos images the depressing and terrifying aspects of the father on all levels: personal, societal, and archetypal. Before this image, youth feels helpless, frightened, immature, and incapable. This is the image that archetypically defines the nature of the rigid, angry father of the boy who killed himself in the movie *Dead Poet's Society*. Later Zeus and his mother combined their efforts to slay Cronos, and after this event, the cycle of son killing father stopped.

But, a more subtle destroyer is the "good father" who has no connection to his own soul. One analysand of mine grew up with a violent, alcoholic father whose favorite pastime was to knock him around while screaming "You're no damn good and you never will be!" My analysand spent the first half of his life as a raging, alcoholic who failed at the critical point in everything he tried: education, marriage, and business. In the second half of life, he sought help and found his destiny as a teacher and therapist. But he claims he found his destiny because of his relationship to his father. Even though it was totally destructive in one sense, their relationship was *alive*. His father, though negative, was there and they encountered each other. Also, my friend learned from his father's abuse that life is difficult and we must struggle. Remember, the defeat of Cronos by Zeus was the beginning of cosmos.

In contrast, the "good" man from a "good" family, who now has his own family, a good business, and a comfortable middle age, is much harder to treat clinically. He is depressed and does not know why because he's done all the right things effectively and done them well. What has happened is that his life force has dried up and sunk into his unconscious. He knows something is wrong but has no idea what and is afraid to risk a deep look or make a drastic change. He does not know how to struggle. He has no courage.

This man probably had a "good" father, a father who paid attention to his grades, attended his ball games, maybe even taught him sports and skills. This son began to believe in himself and to appreciate his father's confidence in him. So what's the problem? The problem often is that the father lived by the cultural and family values he had been indoctrinated into without questioning how they related to his truest nature. If the father lives an unexamined life, if he accepts without question our cultural conventions, then he simply reinforces his son's development of an institutional ego, a substitute identity. In short, such a father may go through the forms, but he is not really there.

The terrible abusive father wounds the soul of a boy. As Robert Bly wrote:

> *Beatings, slaps in the face, verbal batterings are injuries. Blows that lacerate self-esteem, puncture our sense of grandeur, pollute enthusiasm, poison and desolate confidence, give the soul black-and-blue marks, undermining and degrading the body*

*image ... these all make a defilement. They damage
and do harm.*[6]

These wounds may turn out to be beyond repair, or they may
be healed and transformed into sacred wounds, as in the case of my
analysand. But the father who initiates his children into a substitute
identity is another matter. It is much harder to deal with the
existential void, the deep feelings of nonexistence that these men
leave behind. The sons of such men know the silent despair of men
who "die a little every day" as they live unauthentic, unsubstanti-
ated lives. Often they look into themselves and find nothing, even
though they look outward and seem to have a lot, so much that
neither they nor their friends and families understand why something could be wrong. If fate forces us to encounter this wound, as
it invariably does to some of us, then the only thing we can do is take
up the mythic hero's quest to substantiate ourselves.

The moral is that we can survive the encounter with a demon
better than the encounter with a ghost. The paradox is that the
demonic father may express a portion of father love more effectively than the good father. Father love should teach, challenge, and
inspire. But if the father or Fathers haven't attended to their own
spiritual lives, separated their personal values from the cultural
fictions, and developed their own standpoint and character, then
we will continue to virtuously produce new generations of *ghosts.*

Keep in mind that as real relationships have faded and changed
in the past few decades, we have pursued an ever-increasing *ideal*
of what we think they should have been. Often we feel that if our
own relationships with our parents had been "better," we would be
okay. I think it is clear from our discussion so far that the relationships of fathers and children are filled with misunderstandings,
deception, betrayals, concealments, and reversals that, in the end,
form character. To be a father in one way or another is to enter into
deeper community with everyone and everything that exists. At its
best, it is to become a lover of life.

In the movie *Sands of Iwo Jima,* John Wayne played a tough,
relentless Marine sergeant in a role that contributed a lot to the later
stereotyped image of "John Wayne" masculinity. Interestingly, on
his body after he was killed at the end of the movie was an
unfinished letter to his son. It read:

Dear Son,
... always do what your heart tells you is right ...

Reality and Being a Father

After I talked about fatherhood in a men's seminar I was leading a short while ago, one man said, "Boy, you sure have to have your shit together to be a father."

I replied, "If you think so, then you've totally missed the point."

The point is to encounter, to be fully engaged with life and with our children. This is how be a "good enough" father in our own families. From that point we can build toward the value of the FATHER to culture and spirituality.

As both a father and a son, I am most concerned with the human experience of fathering and how we are all affected by the process. But psychologically, behind every father is the archetype of FATHER. This archetype is the ancient, *living psychic force* that dwells eternally in the psychic imagery of humankind, continually shaping and reshaping our evolving consciousness. This is the force that is carried, for better or worse, by our own fathers for awhile, and by us for awhile if we are fathers.

Modern American psychology has been dumbfounded by Jung's concept of the archetype, largely because archetypal images do not yield to specific analysis and into forms and stages. Indeed, if you try to apply such a reductive approach to the archetypes, you destroy their utility in understanding human life. Jung comments:

> *Not for a moment dare we succumb to the illusion that an archetype can be finally explained and disposed of. Even the best attempts at explanation are only more or less successful translations into another metaphorical language.... . The most we can do is to* dream the myth onwards *and give it modern dress.... . The archetype—let us never forget this—is a psychic organ present in all of us.* [7]

It is dangerous to identify with an archetype as we live, because if we do so we lose ourselves to it. But if we consider the archetypal image of FATHER, and try to understand it, it can remain a living psychic force within us. It is in its very abstraction that it can yield hope, information, and the evolution of new patterns of life for us. If we reflect on these images and try to understand their force, they can connect us back to the ancestral intelligence of humankind and lead us into new levels of consciousness in the future.

The archetypal image of the FATHER has stood behind the evolution of the patriarchy and the image of GOD and KING as ruling principles in western culture. And the FATHER image behind the patriarchy is now sick and dying, like the old king in many fairy tales. As we seek to transform and renew this image, we must remember that it has stood for much more than nationalism, war, and the subjugation of women. FATHER-HOOD has also stood for the evolution of consciousness, art, culture, and the manifestations of the spiritual in life. It has stood for law, for healing, and for adventure in the realm of the mind and spirit. If we do away with the masculine spirit, we may lose our respect for the spirituality of life. Man's commitment to values greater than himself is one of the great protectors of the feminine principle, the principle of life and of nature.

As our lives become more complicated and specialized, we must undertake what Eric Neumann called the emotional "reattunement of consciousness." The first step in this reattunement is to evoke again the FATHER image, as we did in Part One of this book. As we struggle to deeply understand the personal and collective nature of fatherhood and its functions and meanings in this part of the book, we will discover that our increasing awareness will compel us to reorient our activities. This is a badly needed infusion of life and energy for fathers as well as for the FATHER image. When things are psychologically disconnected and lifeless, when relationships are dead, only an emotional commitment can restart the flow of energy. The path toward healing and wholeness calls us to release the FATHER image from the bondage of the concretization and the fading abstractions of the old patriarchal heritage. As our journey of understanding deepens, we can develop the archetypal image of the GREAT FATHER more fully as a psychic construct of its own. This image can inform life without the old sociopolitical contaminations prevalent today.

In addition, we need to revive the archetype in the culture of the Fathers. The Fathers in our history have carried two important functions: the training and initiation of young men into adulthood, and shepherding of society and culture. Clearly the Fathers also have become a ghostly institutional abstraction that needs new body and vitality. Without this vitality, we are not going to be able to successfully integrate the new rise in feminine consciousness into our collective life. We already show signs of falling into the opposite pole from where we began a few decades ago and may end up as pathological as when we started.

Archetypal images inform and revitalize us when we are blocked and stymied. They remind us what it means to be alive and human while prompting us to reach for a deeper and fuller experience of life. If we refuse to reduce the image of FATHER to simplistic notions, we can all incorporate the lessons from this image into our own ways, and so learn to live better lives as men and women. When rejected or disowned, FATHERHOOD can become dark, ugly, and consuming—as many forms of the patriarchy are now doing. But when understood and embraced, it can make us whole human beings.

7

Fatherhood and the Courage to Stand for Life

> *Christ, the fulfiller of their prophecies, put an end to this fear of God and taught mankind that the true relationship to the Deity is love. Thus he destroyed the compulsive ceremonial of the law and was himself the exponent of the personal loving relationship to God.*
>
> *... always the order of love transmutes fear and compulsion into a higher freer type of feeling.*
>
> —C. G. Jung

I am struck by how rarely nowadays we hear discussions of the daily choice of good over evil. It sometimes seems that, as our standards for how we act have become pragmatic, reasonable, and realistic, we have narrowed the focus so nobly expressed in the Declaration of Independence down to the pursuit of happiness. In politics, business, and our personal lives, we are justified in becoming players or even observers—in the game of life rather than genuine participants. As our ability to analyze events, situations, and data (unfortunately not ourselves) has increased, our sense of right and wrong has seemed to decrease.

Aleksandr Solzhenitsyn[1] described this trend more than a decade ago as a decline in courage that can be considered a lack of manhood. He credited many of our political ills, both at home and abroad, to a Western world that had lost its "civic courage, both as a whole and separately, in each country, in each government, in each political party, and of course in the United Nations." He attributed the loss of courage and much of the resulting malaise to "spiritual exhaustion" and the evolution, since the Renaissance and the Age of Enlightenment, of "nationalistic humanism" as the foundation of political and social doctrine.

He summarized it this way:

> *The turn introduced by the Renaissance was probably inevitable historically: the Middle Ages had come to a natural end by exhaustion, having become an intolerable despotic repression of man's physical nature in favor of the spiritual one. But then we recoiled from the spirit and embraced all that is material, excessively and incommensurately. The humanistic way of thinking, which has proclaimed itself our guide, did not admit the existence of intrinsic evil in man, nor did it see any task higher than the attainment of happiness on earth. It started modern Western civilization on the dangerous trend of worshiping man and his material needs. Everything beyond physical well-being and the accumulation of material goods, all other human requirements and characteristics of a subtler and higher nature, were left outside the area of attention of state and social systems, as if human life did not have any higher meaning. Thus gaps were left open for evil, and its drafts blow freely today. Mere freedom per se does not in the least solve all the problems of human life and even adds a number of new ones.[2]*

Ironically, he points out that in founding the United States our forefathers considered that:

> *individual human rights were granted on the ground that man is God's creature. That is, freedom was given to the individual conditionally in the assumption of his constant religious responsibility.[3]*

He then proceeds with his conclusion:

> *If, as claimed by humanism, man were born only to be happy, he would not be born to die. Since his body is doomed to death, his task on earth evidently must be more spiritual: not a total engrossment in everyday life, not the search for the best ways to obtain material goods and then their carefree consumption. It has to be the fulfillment of a permanent, earnest duty so that one's life journey may become above all an experience of moral growth: to leave life a better human being than one started it. It is imperative to reappraise the scale of the usual human values; its present incorrectness is astounding.*

So here we are in all our modernity, painfully bouncing back and forth between the opposites of materialistic obsession and a spirituality divorced from life. We have no steadying hand of the father or Fathers guiding us toward courage and balance. In the terms we've been using, the world of the Fathers has lost its courage, the foundation of its strength, and the ability to temper this strength with flexibility, and therefore its vitality. It is failing.

Courage and Aggression Tempered by the Heart

As we evolve away from the patriarchal image of father, we must keep in mind that the king was also the symbolic custodian of the realm, the family, and the personal values of courage and spirituality. As we create new images of fathering, both individually and collectively, we must make sure these new symbols are lived out in our lives. We must each become *citizens* of our world, with all the moral responsibility to the community that citizenship implies. We cannot take this moral responsibility without courage, and we cannot gain courage without understanding the nature of aggression.

Erich Fromm,[4] writing on human destructiveness, classifies aggression into two categories, the first one of which he calls malignant aggression. Malignant aggression attempts to control life by destroying life and the spirit of life. Malignant aggression seeks power—

often as a result of helplessness—violence compensates for impotence and the lack of creativity. Malignant aggression is often paranoid, surrounding itself with defensive walls, hoarding possessions, building up power. In extreme cases, someone, usually a man, tries to get out of the role in which he feels stuck by doing violence to others (the rapist, assassin, terrorist, and mass or serial murderer) or to himself. Much the same thing can happen on a national level.

Fromm's second category of aggression is benign aggression. He felt that aggression could not only be positive as well as negative, but that positive aggression is necessary to life. Positive aggression is often needed to defend and preserve life and includes the spirit of adventure and the use of strength in support of life. The nature of benign aggression fosters life with strength and energy.

Benign aggression is the great legacy of the legends of King Arthur. In these legends, strength was subjected to moral responsibility and used to unite and protect the land and give protection, security, and prosperity to its inhabitants. As this principle increased, it enabled the "Quest for the Holy Grail," the highest spiritual values available to us.

Let us proceed further and see how the notions of malignant and positive or benign aggression are intertwined with fatherhood and our way of life.

Solzhenitsyn characterized "hastiness and superficiality" as the psychic diseases of the twentieth century, and rapid change without depth or direction also can be a form of malignant aggression. Some people think that change is always positive. They feel everything should be open to change—economics, politics, sexuality, gender, and so on. In fact, change often rides on shallow political reasons, feelings of political impotence or inferiority, or a weak, sentimentally idealistic hope to change the human heart by legislation. Jung, in a short article on the Swiss attitude toward the modern world, says:

> *Does neutral Switzerland, with its backward, earthy nature, fulfil any meaningful function in the European system? I think we must answer this question affirmatively. The answer to political or cultural questions need not be only: Progress and Change, but also: Stand still! Hold fast! These days one can doubt in good faith whether the condition*

of Europe shows any change for the better since the war. Opinions, as we know, are very divided, and we have just heard Spengler's lamentations on the decline of the West. Progress can occasionally go downhill, and in the face of a dangerously rapid tempo standing still can be a lifesaver. Nations, too, get tired and long for political and social stabilization. The Pax Romana meant a good deal to the Roman Empire. [5]

In order to combat this form of malignant aggression, the Fathers must *stand for something* in benign aggression. The negative old man or king who simply stands against things destroys the potential for healthy personal and collective growth. Standing against things in this way is a form of malignant aggression and that makes a true relationship with the Self or God impossible, twists our energy from world making to world shaking, and undermines a true respect for the law.

In the movie *Dead Poet's Society*, the father of the boy who wanted to be an actor destroyed his son's potential. Parts of this interchange reflect the malignant process that led to his son's suicide:

"Son, I am trying very hard to understand why you insist on defying us, but whatever the reason, I am not going to let you ruin your life. Tomorrow I am withdrawing you from Welton and enrolling you in Braden Military School. You are going to Harvard and you are going to be a doctor."

Fresh tears welled in Neil's eyes...

"You have opportunities that I never dreamed of!" Mr. Perry shouted. "I won't let you squander them." He stalked out of the room.

Neil stood alone, completely drained of emotion, trying not to think of the future his father had just laid out for him. [6]

Neil's suicide shook their world. This example is extreme, but we do the same thing in many little ways. Fathers in this trap confuse conventional values, rigidity, and obeying rules with maturity and responsibility. To live with true responsibility to our inner nature in a way that insures an authentic life with value and meaning may require a great deal of positive aggression in standing for life.

Fathers who stand for life in benign aggression protect and channel the developing energies of their children or culture. They help these energies to mature without being swept away in the modern wave of anxiety and shallowness. "Hastiness and superficiality," one of the most subtle forms of malignant aggression, alienate us from matters of the *heart*. Fathers can protect us from them.

As malignant aggression spreads through modern life, money and possessions replace eros. We develop a trader's mentality, thinking only in terms of debits or credits. We ask ourselves, "How much will it cost?" whether we're making a purchase, considering a divorce, getting our kid out of a scrape, or wondering about cheating on our taxes. Even Christianity, influenced almost from its beginning by St. Paul in the trader's format, has evolved from a religion of love, passion, suffering, and desire to one of membership drives and increased pledges, TV ads, and pitchman's tactics. Good intentions are no protection against this insidious attack, since greed always destroys the good it promises to deliver. The man and wife who want the best for their families may buy so many things, and have their children enrolled in so many of the best schools, sports, and activities that they are hopelessly overburdened financially. As a result, they are constantly overworked and overstressed. In desperation, they try to get more and spend more to ease their anguish—including expensive psychiatric treatment, therapeutic camps, and drug treatment centers for their children. Unless they luck into some insightful psychotherapist who isn't caught in the same trap or have some eye-opening life experience, they never realize they've slipped into a cycle of greed masked by proper-sounding goals. These seemingly good parents think they work hard and suffer unjustly, but they won't admit, even to themselves, that it was greed that incited them to assume these burdens.

In archetypal terms, money is connected to VALUE, the feeling side of life, the part of us that evaluates the worth of situations and relationships. When our feeling side is neglected (as often happens in modern education), we can easily confuse the conventional symbol of value–money–with value itself. Money and greed, or the other side of the same coin, gambling and extravagance, become compulsive and addictive.

In order to keep the symbol of value from becoming a value in itself, we Fathers have to discover genuine values. And once again courage enters the picture. We must search for our real values and separate them from what Alfred Adler called our "fictions." Some of our leading fictions are that things such as science, technology, capitalism, democracy, and individualism are good, or at least lead to a better life. Competition is another American icon, and we seem to insist that it is healthy, strengthens character, and, in business, is more effective in every situation.

All of these things are no doubt good, but Jung helped us to understand that no matter how good something is, it also has a darker side. We must learn to look courageously at the dark side of our cultural fictions and to reflect on what we have done, what we are doing, and what our activities and their underlying attitudes mean. According to the Jungian Analyst and scholar Marie-Louise von Franz:

> *America is too sentimental. Freedom ... democracy for everybody, world police looking for order ... This is a rose-colored sentimentality that is the shadow of brutality.*[7]

Alfred Adler (a psychoanalyst who, like Jung, developed his own theories) concluded that our fictions enable us to deal more effectively with the world, both in hoping for a future and as compensation for psychological wounding in the past. He also concluded that aggression was more important than sexuality. In other words, he thought that aggression resulting from feelings of inferiority is the driving force of human behavior. Adler also thought that

> *the normal person could free himself from the influence of fictions and face reality when necessity demanded, something the neurotic person is incapable of doing.*[8]

Our culture is beginning to become aware of fictions like the above, but do we have the political courage to change them? I have already pointed out that fostering the self-confidence that underlies political courage is one function of personal fathers and the Fathers. I have also noted that the covert spiritual instruction that our children get from institutions undermines this self-confidence. If confidence is based on competition instead of mastery, as is so often the case in our schools, our sense of confidence and competence is always built on a foundation of sand. If someone must always lose, we know it will eventually be us. In Adlerian terms, *feelings of inferiority* and the compensatory *striving for superiority* become an endless cycle. The more we succeed, the more we fear failure, and the more we fight to succeed. This cycle murders the human soul.

This cycle also prevents genuine success. Ironically, the most successful businessmen I know are not the most cutthroat. They are the ones who have learned to express their creativity and themselves through business. They are on their own path and are not distracted by the negativity around them.

What can one father do? If we look at our vast social system, it may not seem like we can do much. But one father can share his values, struggles, and beliefs with his children. By doing this, he can counteract the influence of institutions, and help them develop a critical consciousness. And interacting with them will also help us develop our own values, since adolescents are only too happy to point out what's wrong with our society.

We need the spirit of adventure–a form of benign aggression–in order to take this open approach to life. As we examine our cultural fictions, we may find we need to break cultural traditions to do things like starting new businesses and pursuing more Spartan but meaningful careers. It may cost us possessions or social status, but in order for our children to develop the love of life as a principle, they need security, justice, and the freedom to create, to venture, and to wander. Material well-being can only provide, at best, the suffocating kind of security that kills freedom in the end. Our children need security that gives them a sense of optimism and hope about life, and that can only come from fathers who follow their hearts.

The quiet and gentle dignity of the Dali Lama illustrates how standing for the human heart and compassion can bring self-confidence. His example of self-discipline has become a source of meaning for himself and his followers. His religion is a form of connectedness with the creative force of life, and when we are connected to life in this way, we can safely act from our hearts. We respond naturally to the needs of life, reaching out to heal a hurt without needing to think about it. When we lose this connectedness, we need a code of ethics to tell us the proper thing to do, and as life becomes more complicated and less personal, our ethical system becomes more abstract. Our "shoulds" and "oughts" become removed from human needs and our religion becomes a creed to be defended rather than a relationship to be lived. The spiritual life, true life, still comes out of self-knowledge, the search for truth, integration, and wholeness. True action in the service of the spirit of life comes from this same source.

As fathers develop the courage to allow themselves to know and be known, to stand for their values, and to welcome the equality of their maturing children, they will model benign aggression for their children. The heroic men in the past (Christ, Martin Luther King, Jr., Gandhi, Anwar Sadat and others) have given us a model of how to transform courage from conquering others to preserving life and pursuing the inner journey. They have given us a "sword," the mythical symbol of masculine consciousness and discrimination—in the name of life. We must pick up this sword and use it to discriminate between benign and malignant aggression, to transform heroic courage from conquering to preserving life, and finally to fully understand the reality of our culture. Fathers must pick up this sword and wield it against the dragons and beasts in our society.

What about courage and aggression in personal relationships? In my experience as an analyst, women seem to be hungering for positive male aggression. The most common complaint I have heard from women is, "He won't fight with me."

Of course, this doesn't mean that women want a man who will knock their teeth in. But what these women have are men who either explode or just quietly withdraw in the face of confrontation. This withdrawal is often itself a form of aggression, but a lot of men are genuinely confused by the difference between benign and malignant aggression. Many of these men have no repertoire between giving in and turning brutal. When their emotions heat up, they either explode or walk out. After all, men are brought up to be objective, concrete, and rational, and this training doesn't apply very well to their emotional lives. At their worst, these men say, "Yes, dear, whatever you say, dear," and then do exactly as they please. In relationships this behavior is malignant aggression.

A man with love and spirit also can openly get angry and argue with his girlfriend, his wife, his children, or even his boss. A man who has faced his terror, who has been initiated and is out from under the patriarchal image, can reclaim his emotions, even his anger, while continuing to stand for both his values and eros. He can listen to and share emotions, even at the top of his lungs. He can allow himself to be moved and touched by others, responding to their needs while maintaining his own integrity.

Most therapists know that men who have a hard time relating to women also will have a hard time relating to their children. A number of books are currently in print about the yearning of men to have intimacy with their fathers. I think deep down inside we all yearn for intimacy, but to find it we need courage, a spirit of adventure and action in the service of living. In short, we need benign aggression.

8

A Heart of Flame: Transformation and the Transcendent Father

Freud was of the opinion that all "divine" figures have their roots in the father-imago.

—C. G. Jung

Robert Bly and others have pointed out that masculine images in our culture have been decaying for some time. Bly made the following observations on Zeus, the Greek Father God who could be said to represent a projection of the FATHER archetype in early Greek culture:

> *There's a general assumption now that every man in a position of power is or soon will be corrupt and oppressive. Yet the Greeks understood and project a positive male energy that has accepted authority. They call it Zeus energy, which encompasses intelligence, robust health, compassionate decisiveness, good will, generous leadership. Zeus energy is male authority accepted for the sake of the community.[1]*

We can see how far this archetypal image of FATHER and FATHER energy has decayed by looking at another view of Zeus. In her book *Gods in Everyman: A New Psychology of Men's Lives and*

Loves, Dr. Jean Bolen, a psychiatrist and Jungian analyst, heads a section in her chapter on Zeus, "Zeus the Philanderer."[2] She describes a number of his "affairs" and "seductions" such as when Zeus became a shower of gold to impregnate Danaë, whose son then became the hero Perseus. She then goes on to describe Zeus as a "sky god"–a bisexual, power driven, distant, controlling philanderer. She gives him a few points for being decisive, having vision, and making alliances, but for the most part, her Zeus is simply the stereotype of all the worst characteristics of the male psyche.

This makes one wonder where Robert Bly got his information. How did Bly and Bolen come up with two such different perspectives? Perhaps for the sake of balance, we should look at what scholars in other fields have said. In their *Classical Mythology*, M. P. O. Marford and R. J. Lenardon tell us:

> *It is important to realize as well that Zeus becomes the god who upholds the highest moral values in the order of the universe—values that he absorbs unto himself or that are divided among and shared by other deities. He is the god who protects the family, the clan, and the state, championing the universal moral and ethical responsibilities that these human associations entail. He protects suppliants, imposes ties of hospitality, upholds the sanctity of oaths; in a word he is the defender of all that is right.[3]*

And as to Zeus being only a sky-god, Walter Burkert in his *Greek Religion* says:

> *Zeus was the only god who could become an all-embracing god of the universe. The tragedians did not present him on stage, in contrast to Athena, Apollo, Artemis, Aphrodite, Hera, and Dionysus. Aeschylus names Zeus alone, far above all other gods, with predicates of universality: all-powerful, all-accomplisher, and cause of all; "ruler of rules, most blessed of the blessed, of the perfected most perfect power, happy Zeus," one of his lost tragedies*

*proclaimed: "Zeus is aether, Zeus is earth, Zeus is
sky, Zeus is everything and what is still higher
than this." In Dodona the priestesses sang: "Zeus
was, Zeus is, Zeus will be: O great Zeus," while a
line of Orpheus announced: "Zeus is beginning,
Zeus is middle, from Zeus are all things finished."
Here the philosophical speculation which
culminated in the pantheism of the Stoics could
find its beginnings: Zeus is the world as a whole,
and especially the thinking fire which pervades
everything, forms everything, and holds everything
in limits.* [4]

As we try to revitalize masculinity, we must not fall prey to our
fear that life is not concretely and rationally controllable. When we
succumb to this fear, we often try to control the uncontrollable by
putting labels on it and making these labels the coin of our
experience. If we do this, we ignore the symbolic characteristics of
such things as the Zeus myths and the infinite gradations of values
they represent. We wind up with an illusion of control when in fact
we are missing reality altogether. We are, as a friend of mine says,
"simply going deeper into shallowness."

Images and the way we perceive them make up the "eyes of our
mind." We have to look beyond the concrete appearance of things
to the mythical and subjective aspect of images, or we fail to
comprehend human REALITY. If we fall prey to our anxiety and
shallowness, we forfeit our true identity without being conscious of
what we're doing. Our real masculinity and femininity are lost by
a servile surrendering of all that is most human, noble, and decent
within ourselves.

If we look to the images behind the myths, we find that Zeus
is not being promiscuous when he impregnates Danaë. Their
union is a metaphor for the highest spiritual value (gold symbolizes sun-glory, self-generating radiance, freedom from decay,
immortality, spiritual luminosity, and so on all over the world)
joining the feminine principle of matter. Campbell refers to this
type of metaphorical image as the "incarnation of spirit in
matter." This union has an extremely creative result, the birth of
the hero or the divine child. To reduce this lovely, powerful

metaphor to a one-night stand by a promiscuous executive, as
Bolen does, is psychic idolatry and undermines the inner work
of Jungian psychology.

Zeus's "promiscuity" has symbolic meaning far beyond the
literal acts described in the myths. Rollo May[5] pointed out that
the original Greek and Hebrew words meaning "to know" also
meant "to have sexual relations." Knowledge itself, as well art,
is a result of the dynamic encounter between two opposite
characteristics. Creativity occurs in this act of encounter, and the
dynamics may be understood as the center of the creative
process. The liaisons of Zeus can be taken to stand for metaphorically the archetypal processes of creativity. The double
meaning of the word also implicates that as sexual relations, acts
of creativity are both instinctual and passionate. And the knowledge contained in the word suggests both inner knowledge and
the direct knowledge of living experience.

Creativity, living creatively, brings us into life, and into a
world which is always starting anew. The creative inspirations of
Greek culture still affect us in almost every field of human
endeavor. I still marvel at their art, their painting, their poetry,
and their literature. I wonder what we are creating that will
inspire awe in the human soul two thousand years from now.

Nor do Zeus and his relationships illustrate a power-hungry
man taking advantage of women. These *metaphors* show the
many ways that the creative masculine principle, logos, came
together with the receptive feminine principle, eros, to bring
about new life. And the receptivity of the feminine, as symbolized by the women in the myths, has nothing to do with passivity.
They reflect the creative person holding himself or herself open,
or being held open by the power of their creative passion, to
whatever may emerge. This act entails patience and includes
gestation and is often difficult. Both the masculine and feminine
principles take an active part in the act of creativity by which we
humans express our being.

The episode of Zeus and Ganymede, from the standpoint of
metaphor, has little to do with homosexuality. Symbolically it
suggests enough self-knowledge to stay in contact with the
eternal adolescent. The old man and the youth has been a major
theme both throughout this book and in the mythology of men

in general. The ruling principles always need the challenging, renewing, life-demanding attitude of youth. Ganymede becomes Zeus's cupbearer and is later immortalized in the constellation Aquarius as the water-bearer, the bearer of spirit, change and renewal.

Furthermore, archetypal images are numinous, transcendent, and mysterious. They represent values that are beyond our full comprehension, as we are also finding out with the image of the Great Mother. Amplifying the archetypal images can deepen our knowledge of them and can psychologically inform us. It is clear that Zeus was an image radiating numinosity, the mystery of the masculine and father principles, and the power of logos that can create and hold cosmos. This image once inspired respect, wonder, and fascination. If we amplify this image, we gain a sense of the potential power of development in the human being. Likewise, we have some idea of how little we have developed our own psychological potential.

As we study mythology, we also can see how the archetypal images evolve and mature as humankind evolves. Zeus grows more mature as the literature and poetry of ancient Greece develop. Aeschylus has Hephaestus say at one point that Zeus has only recently become ruler and that "everyone is harsh when he first comes to power." Commenting on this, Marford and Lenardon say: The contrast is presumably with the later Zeus who will have learned benevolence through experience, wisdom, and maturity.[6]

After defeating his father and the Titans Zeus seems almost post-adolescent. He has symbolically overcome the barbarous nature of both of them and brought it under the control of consciousness. Later, as illustrated in *The Odyssey*, Zeus seems to have matured, showing compassion and a sense of justice and unity as he supports Odysseus in his final quests.

Jahweh follows a similar course of development in the Old Testament. Like Zeus, he seemed to have to struggle with other heavenly beings and his own emotions before the cosmic order could be put fully in place. Once this task was in balance, he could change his focus to that of structuring humanity's development. However, the Old Testament God goes a step further, renewing himself, humankind, and the relationship of spirit and matter through his son. This is one of the greatest archetypal patterns of renewal that deepens the eternal symbolic relationship of the father and the son.

Kingship — Nobility of the Human Spirit

The images of gods, goddesses, kings, and queens in religions, myths, and legends also reflect humankind's continuous struggle to rise above themselves, to be *noble*. The image of the king represents more than order, it represents the nobility of the human spirit.

Helen Luke describes kingship psychologically as follows:

> *... a king will be true to his kingship insofar as he is faithful to the "best," never substituting the second best, never identifying his ego with his royalty. If he interprets his great inheritance from the ancestors in the light of the "best" of his own age, he then becomes the symbol, not only of the stored riches of the past, but of the new consciousness of the present and of that which gives birth to the hidden seed of the future, the heir to the throne.*[7]

Luke goes on to suggest that each of us must continually ask ourselves what kind of ruler is in charge of our personality. Is he a king of royal blood or a mere demagogue or politician elected to serve the moment, our ego, our parents, or society? She also points out that having a king is important in a woman's psyche.

> *The king in a woman's psyche is not substantially different from his image in a man's. He is for her, as for him, the leading principle of her being to which she gives allegiance, but he manifests himself in different ways. Obviously, a woman who is possessed by a multiplicity of animi has not found the king at all. She spends her life in the atmosphere of a party convention, proclaiming the inalienable truth of one set of opinions and denouncing all who oppose them; or else she is at the mercy of her emotions, bending to every wind that blows, unable*

to utter a clear "yes" or "no." But if she has found
an objective truth that is her *truth for any given*
time of her life and has the courage to live by it, she
has found the king, and he will show himself in her
life rather in a great enrichment of her femininity
than in a wielding of the sword in her outer life.
For the animus, whether king or commoner, is for
a woman that which relates her to her unconscious
mind; and the king in her psyche must indeed take
up, or reforge, his sword, but he wields it in the
service of her creativity in the inner *world; and so*
her function of true feminine relatedness is freed
from the plots by which it is distorted when her
inferior masculinity rules from below without a
true king to lead and command. Then, if this is her
way, she can enter the masculine world with a
creative strength of spirit peculiarly her own.[8]

(Incidentally, the image of the queen is just as important for
men and women psychologically, but that is not the subject of
this book. If you'd like to read a good amplification of this figure,
I recommend Helen Luke's work.)

We also can see the nobility of kingship reflected in the oldest
tale recorded in the English language, Beowulf. The tale begins
with Beowulf as a young hero going to a foreign land to help an
old king slay a monster from the deep, and then the monster's
mother. The legend is clear that Beowulf had to grow into his
destiny and that he was not born to heroism. He had to come to
grips with the first monster hand to hand; then with the mother
monster (the evil side of maternalism), he had to rise above
himself and slay her with a giant's sword. Up to this point, this
is a classic hero's tale, and Beowulf wins his identity, glory,
rewards, and sword.

But this tale goes on. Beowulf returns to his homeland,
demonstrates emotional maturity by his generous and courteous
behavior, marries, and humbly becomes the king in his own
land. The end of this tale is the most interesting to me. In this part
of the tale we find Beowulf an older man recalling his grandfather's
troubles and his uncles' fratricide. We have the image of the

aging king trying to get his life into focus as he faces his impending death. In his final battle, he fights a fearful dragon, with only the help of a *young man*, to rid the land of this monster and obtain its treasure for his people, showing that generosity is as vital to good kingship as courage. In this final scene, he is the old yet courageous hero-king, motivated only by the desire to protect and provide for his people. He wins his final battle and loses his life in the process.

Yet even though Beowulf leaves his people a treasure, they do not live happily ever after. The messenger who brings the news of the king's death points out that the land is in danger of invasion and fragmentation because the king is dead. So the cycle of life goes on: Threats, conflict, and fragmentation issue the call for a new king, and the land must bear the conflict until a new one is found or developed.

Courage and generosity evolved further to include compassion, justice, mercy, and eros in the legends of King Arthur. The Grail King, according to Joseph Campbell, was "the guardian of the highest spiritual values—compassion and loyalty." Also, we find in these legends the beginning of the modern version of the individual quest to heal the Grail King and the Wasteland that results when the guardian of the highest spiritual values is wounded.

We now see that kingship in its positive light symbolizes the best in humanity. Nobility holds together the inner realm of mind and heart, desire and justice, strength and mercy, and joins them with responsibility. To revitalize the king, we must meet and struggle with our own dark nature as Parzival fought with his dark brother Feirefiz on his final approach to the Grail Castle. Campbell noted that after they recognized each other they sat down and "began talking about their father."[9]

As we saw in the stories of Zeus and Beowulf, the king must mature. When the hero has succeeded in his fight against the established power, the negative father in the case of Zeus and the devouring mother in case of Beowulf, he becomes king and a new cycle begins. The hero must change, he must marry the feminine principle and become a creative and constructive ruler, organizing, reforming, and providing security. As he ages, his creative and dynamic drives give way to conservative values and he becomes more protective.

Gradually the king's creativity becomes stale and his established order stifles new development. If he has been wise and has sufficiently honored the feminine, a new prince may be ready to assume the throne. If not, another hero will have to come forth to do battle with him and establish a new order. but while even new figures must fill the throne, the office of kingship as a symbol of man's nobility goes on. Kings come and go. Kingship is eternal.

There is still another level of kingship, that of Christ, the "king of kings." Here is an even higher level of consciousness bringing a rule of love and compassion that surpasses the mind of man and even so-called divine law. Here the archetypal relationship of the father and the son becomes transcendent, manifested by spirit incarnated in matter, in "the only Son of God, eternally begotten of the Father."

There is a negative image of the king as well in the image of Herod the Great. Greed, impotence, and the loss of the noble principles foster the murderous, demonic king who savages any form of new life and creativity. It is also interesting to note that the Pax Romana, peace achieved through order with no personal spiritual connection to the people involved, supported the reign of Herod. As our culture becomes more abstract and secular and our noblest ideals and spirituality fade into the mists, we run the risk of creating and supporting many Herods—as we already have in this century.

All of this talk about gods, kings, myths, and legends may seem a little off track. But I am surprised by the number of men and women I have met who have no sense of the nobility of human nature. For them, following their bliss is a matter of satisfying their egos, if they can find their egos at all. The old stories still carry the great themes of humanity, and it is the function of the Fathers to pass them on as *touchstones* for our development.

The recordings of the stories of the Cherokees in the Cherokee Museum in North Carolina begin in this lovely way:

These stories come from a long time ago, shortly after creation, when the spirit of every living thing walked on the face of the earth. This is what the old men told me a long time ago.

And the psalmist tells us (Ps. 78):

> *What we have heard and known,*
> *What our fathers have told us.*
> *We will not hide them from our children;*
> *We will tell the next generation ...*

The Dual Nature of FATHERHOOD — Authority Versus AUTHORITY

In the story of the rich young man,[10] a rich young man addresses Jesus as "Good teacher" and asks what he must do to have eternal life. Jesus, after declining to be called "good," asks the young man whether he has kept the commandments, and he replies he's kept them all. Then Jesus tells him to sell everything and to follow him. The man becomes sad and walks away. Jesus goes on to speak of the difficulty of the rich entering the kingdom of God, using the famous example of a camel passing though the eye of a needle. He then said, "what is impossible for men is possible with God." The story continues:

> *"I tell you the truth," Jesus said to them, "no one*
> *who has left home or wife or brothers or parents or*
> *children for the sake of the kingdom of God will*
> *fail to receive many times as much in this age and,*
> *in the age to come, eternal life."*

Several points in this story illustrate the dual nature of the FATHER and FATHER authority. The young man had done everything right in his life. He was a success, he was virtuous, and he seemed to be an ideal man for his time. He had followed the rules of the paternal authority of his era for developing his identity, consciousness, and place in the world–he had followed the way of the Fathers. No doubt his mother was proud of him, also. Yet he had a yearning for something else–eternal life, completeness.

The psalmist (42) speaks of yearning this way:

> *Like the deer that yearns for the running streams,*
> *so my soul is yearning for you, my God. My soul is*
> *thirsting for God, the God of my life; when can I*
> *enter and see the face of God? Tears have become my*

bread by night, by day ...

I have seen exactly this situation when men or women who seem to have it all come into analysis. Sometimes they feel a yearning and a vague sense of discontent. Sometimes they have been struggling longer and their yearning is expressed in depression, addiction, promiscuity, or some other type of illness. They have identified with their role, followed the conventional wisdom of the Fathers, but something deeper in them has become disturbed. They are still seeking eternal life.

One such man had the following dream.

> *A funeral procession is bearing my corpse to the gravesite. The casket is being drawn by horses and somber funeral music is being played. When the casket arrives at the gravesite, Dr. Jung, who is very old, is there. He says that this is the case of a young man who was never able to shed his persona mask. As a result, he died prematurely because he tried to live a false life.*
>
> *I am hearing all of this even though my body is dead. My mind is still alive. I ask Dr. Jung if there is still a chance for me to live. He says that if I try hard enough I may be able to even though my body is dead.*

Note that the first thing Christ does is refuse to be called "good." Thus he dissociates himself from the conventional wisdom of the Fathers and the approval of the Mothers. He goes on to point out that this young man must give up his attachments to his role, his success, and his family. He must break up his vision of how life should be. According to Erich Neumann, he must make the heroic choice to become a conscious individual and answer the call of the Transpersonal FATHER which is in apparent conflict with the conventional wisdom of the Fathers. Neumann goes on to explain it this way:

> *... the hero has to "awaken the sleeping images of the future which can and must come forth from the night, in order to give the world a new and better*

face." This necessarily makes him a breaker of the old law. He is the enemy of the old ruling system, of the old cultural values and the existing court of conscience, and so he necessarily comes into conflict with the fathers and their spokesman, the personal father.

In this conflict the "inner voice," the command of the transpersonal father or father archetype who wants the world to change, collides with the personal father who speaks for the old law. We know this conflict best from the Bible story of Jehovah's command to Abraham: "Get thee out of thy country, and from thy kindred, and from thy father's house, unto a land that I will show thee" (Genesis 12:1), which the Midrash interprets as meaning that Abraham is to destroy the gods of his father. The message of Jesus is only an extension of the same conflict, and it repeats itself in every revolution. Whether the new picture of God and the world conflicts with an old picture, or with the personal father, is unimportant, for the father always represents the old order and hence also the old picture current in his cultural canon.

Observe that God said "into a land that I will show thee." He did not inform Abraham in advance where that would be. Abraham needed trust and courage to make his journey. If he knew where he was going, it would simply be a trip.

In studying psychology we find that there is an intimate bond between the words "conscious" and "responsibility," two words continually connected to the FATHER archetype in all its levels of meaning. This bond is clear in languages such as French and English, which employ words with a common root to express "consciousness" and "conscience." Conscience is a concept closely akin to responsibility, and it is in this sense that we refer to an initiated person as a self-responsible adult. Our understanding of self-responsibility only began as the second millennium B.C. faded into the first. This is when the great philosophers and teachers of East and West discovered "spirit," and this discovery began a dim awareness of the person and *personal* responsibilities.

Becoming a self-responsible adult is the first level of the heroic journey. On this level the conventional wisdom of the Fathers, their rules and guidelines, play an important part. These rules and guidelines usually inform what we normally consider the super-ego. As we pursue the journey of individuation further, we must answer the call of the Transcendent FATHER (the Great Life Giver) to become one of the Life Givers. For this we must proceed to a deeper, or higher, level of consciousness and responsibility beyond the social character of the Fathers.

In order to reach the Transcendent Father we must be willing to embrace paradox, to sell all that we have to gain what we want. We must follow the tortuous path of not releasing the tension but living the contradictions, fully and painfully aware of the poles between which our lives are being stretched. If we have the courage to allow ourselves to be plunged into the paradox rather than walking away sadly, at the center we will find transcendence and new life. We will find a resolution beyond what we could have foreseen or even imagined. Christ assures us that we will be rewarded both in this age and the next.

We need to rely on metaphors and symbols to get us through such personal crises. If we try to view ourselves intellectually, carefully weighing the alternatives before we decide whether or not eternal life is worth what we own, we end up split from ourselves rather than deepened in our self-knowledge, and no matter how well we have "adjusted," we feel a vague sense of dissatisfaction, a feeling that something is lacking, and a yearning we do not understand. Metaphorically, we are still yearning for the spiritual FATHER. We long for transcendence. The popular tendency has been to think of transcendence as an upward and outward escape from the unpleasant, mundane realities of ourselves and our world. Instead, transcendence is a breaking-in, a breathing of the spirit into the heart of our existence. It does involve forces beyond our understanding, whether we call them God, the Self, our higher power, or something else. But transcendence doesn't take us out of ourselves, it makes us more ourselves. If we study mysticism, we find that the mystic way brings us more fully into what Evelyn Underhill called the REALITY beyond the literal reality of our roles and ordinary lives.

Transcendence is the power to be born anew, to make a fresh

start. By suffering the tension of the opposites, we can enter a state of grace on a new level of consciousness. Often in the course of these transformations, we have a feeling of coming home to ourselves and developing a new life that is more in tune with what is highest in us, our nobility. This process is more than just an emotional experience. It is a realignment of all dimensions of ourselves with the deeper source of our life. In the mythic hero's journey this is the stage of atonement (at-one-ment) with the FATHER.

Instead of changing our situation, we begin to change ourselves, or allow ourselves to be changed. Viktor Frankl expressed this notion beautifully:

> *I thereby understand the primordial anthropological fact that being human is being always directed, and pointing, to something or someone other than oneself: to a meaning to fulfill or another human being to encounter, a cause to serve or a person to love. Only to the extent that someone is living out this self-transcendence of human existence, is he truly human or does he become his true self. He becomes so, not by concerning himself with his self's actualization, but by forgetting himself and giving himself, overlooking himself and focusing outward. Consider the eye, an analogy I am fond of invoking. When, apart from looking in a mirror, does the eye see anything of itself? An eye with a cataract may see something like a cloud, which is its cataract; an eye with glaucoma may see its glaucoma as a rainbow halo around the lights. A healthy eye sees nothing of itself—it is self-transcendent.*
>
> *What is called self-actualization is, and must remain, the unintended effect of self-transcendence; it is ruinous and self-defeating to make it the target of intention. And what is true of self-actualization also holds for identity and happiness. It is the very "pursuit of happiness" that obviates happiness. The more we make it a target, the more widely we miss.* [12]

As we come in more direct contact with the ultimate REAL-ITY, what had been a psychological task becomes a spiritual quest. We do not release ourselves from the fetters of law and convention (our cultural Father and Mother), but instead we discover the ultimate source of the law (the Transcendent FA-THER) within the depth of our own personalities. The spiritual quest of the FATHER is to inspire passionate, creative, and authentic living. The image of Christ leads us to live the conflicts and our destiny with acceptance and resolve. Often we may feel that we are in a Garden of Gethsemane, but this is a major reason that the Fathers need to initiate us into courage through ordeals. If we take the way of ease, searching instead for the Garden of Eden, we become victims of fate.

Grandfather — The Wise Old Man

Once we have met the Great Father we see life through a different eye. We see REALITY and the source of life beyond the conflict, pain, suffering, and chaos of the world. We have reached the archetype of the WISE OLD MAN. As Joseph Campbell puts it:

> *The problem of the hero going to meet the father is to open his soul beyond terror to such a degree that he will be ripe to understand how the sickening and insane tragedies of this vast and ruthless cosmos are completely validated in the majesty of Being. The hero transcends life with its peculiar blind spot and for a moment rises to a glimpse of the source. He beholds the face of the father, understands—and the two are atoned.* [13]

The wise old man has lived through the hero cycle and he has lived life. From his years of life he has learned that

> *The living waters are the tears of God. Herewith the world discrediting insight of the monk, "All life is sorrowful," is combined with the world begetting affirmative of the father: "Life must be!"* [14]

The wise old man embodying the above insight is an archetypal symbol of both wisdom and wholeness. He is also the image of the unity of masculine development assimilating all the components of masculine maturity. Wisdom is no longer a ghost without strength and courage. Mature compassion has found a power beyond mere sentimentality.

The wise old man stands rooted in the masculine principle close to the GREAT FATHER archetype, but he also has integrated his anima, or feminine self. She is in her proper place, connecting him to his own depths. We can see this integration in the development of the seer Tiresias in Greek literature. Tiresias gained his powers of knowledge and prophecy from Zeus and through an encounter with a snake (an old symbol of the renewal of consciousness) and the intervention of Hera and Zeus, Tiresias actually lived as both a man and a woman. Also, the wise old man is often presented in myth and legend as blind, which shows that his inner vision is more intense and his insight more acute. Likewise, he may live outside society, in the forest or a cave, giving him a distant and more objective vantage point on society. Tiresias was blind and he lived outside of the social confines, sometimes in the country and he was often consulted in the underworld.

The old man stands for personal responsibility, as Tiresias told Oedipus to "put your own house in order." Tiresias also stood for facing our own inner truth as he again told Oedipus, "Your enemy is yourself." And in addition, he realized the value of suffering as he remarked, "To be wise is to suffer."

In contrast to the wise old man is the wise old woman, who continues to be rooted in the feminine principle near to the GREAT MOTHER archetype. The wise old woman offers the wisdom and creativity as well as the destructive power of nature. When we approach the wise old man, we approach the source of our own truth. When we approach the wise old woman, we approach the source of our own nature.

The wise old man has enormous wisdom and inner strength. He can see the truth beyond our rational minds and beyond the muddle of today's problems, and is often portrayed as a mystic. What happens to this image in a society that centers itself around youth? According to E. F. Schumacher:

World crises multiply and everybody deplores the

shortage, or even total lack, of "wise" men or women, unselfish leaders, trustworthy counselors, etc. It is hardly rational to expect such high qualities from people who have never done any inner work *and would not even understand what is meant by the words.* [15]

The older person in our society is caught between the specter of decline and the dream of eternal youth. As a result, most older people usually either despair or go into denial, and the culture loses the embodiment of the wise old man archetype. As this powerful archetype becomes a ghost and the positive images of the masculine spirit (power, wisdom, and love) are lost, they join the personal and collective shadow. Then they are expressed in their negative form (impotence, ignorance, and hate) in *malignant aggression.*

In addition, we lose the leavening power of the Grandfathers in society. The function of the Fathers is to establish and maintain law and order, while the Grandfathers are society's mystics. We need the grandfathers to inform and open our heart. The Fathers give us the form for living. The Grandfathers give us the dynamics for the *art of living.* In their absence we have little to give our children in the way of a vision of the world, of high models of living and a profound sense of connection with life and others. The wise old man stands for civilization in the highest sense and without him, much of the best of civilization is lost.

In the classic movie I mentioned earlier, *She Wore a Yellow Ribbon,* John Wayne played an old soldier who pointed out that it was the job of old men not to retire and go fishing but to *prevent wars.* We need this balancing voice of wisdom and vitality if our culture is to go beyond itself and to keep alive the voice of the Great Life Givers. We need this voice of higher AUTHORITY to *leaven* the voice of the Fathers.

When we offer Christ's peace we are not speaking of the simple peace of order or harmony (the peace of the Fathers) and certainly not the wishful peace of sentimentalists. We have already seen that Pax Romana fostered Herod. We are speaking of being at peace with the source of life and accepting the conflict and suffering of transcendent living—of individuation.

We do not have to become great seers and sages to find this

peace. John Wayne was an army captain in the above movie. We can be teachers, professionals, farmers, laborers, and personal fathers. All we have to do is "know what we are doing." Then we will include the voice of the Great Life Givers in our own lives and it will pass into the world in a ripple effect. The great deed is not out in the world but within ourselves, and each of us contributes to reforming the world by facing our own inner challenges. The wise old man, through his wisdom, patience, strength, and compassion, transforms ordinary living to the art of living.

Suffering and Grief

"The living waters are the tears of God." The wise old man and the wise old woman share the one great human condition of suffering. We no longer pay much attention to the fact that life is always difficult and requires grief. The problem is not just that we had distant fathers but that we have lost our connection to the tradition of the FATHERS, to the source of life and of the pain of life. Our distance from the FATHERS has left a void that we often fill with the illusion that life can be conquered (in a shallow way) and should be easy and happy. Life always engenders grief, and we must realize that.

Often the first grief we encounter in the growth process has to do with those wonderful adolescent dreams we had of life–or those we did not have because parental-societal expectations ground our spirits to dust at an early age. We may be grieving for that marvelous adolescent energy that we were never quite able to actualize or that we may have buried in shyness or depression or constantly felt we had to sacrifice in little ways in order to become adults. Maybe under the "eyes" of adults we separated from our King, losing touch with the best within us, or went away like the prodigal son without our father's blessing and never found our way home again.

Maybe we grieve because we've never quite impressed the man or woman (inner or outer) as much as we would have liked to, never fully enjoyed or even been able to enjoy their love and admiration. Possibly we are still yearning for the transcendent, for God, for the spiritual FATHER, and to be one of the Great Life Givers.

Our grief is complex and suffering goes with being fully alive.

We need to be able to weep, lament, and mourn the process of life. And we need to be able to dance and sing with our frustration and grief with life and God. We also need to be careful that we do not get fixated in the latest psychological fashions for grief, carefully ticking off the various stages of grief as defined by the latest self-help books. We simply need to grieve, and to reclaim that dimension of being human.

Summary — Seven Houses of the Father

In Jungian analysis, the major process we use is dialogue with the other person. As we do our inner work, we also dialogue with personifications, images, figures from myths or dreams and other metaphors. This dialogue requires us to develop some distance from the part of ourselves we are working with in order to relate to it, and this distance leads to a certain amount of objectivity. Also as we look more deeply at each image or metaphor, we find it leads us to something else. The deeper we go, the more we find that all things possess the potentiality for meaning. Most of us begin our personal exploration by assuming that we are the authors of our destiny. We think we have simply strayed onto the wrong path, need a better "map" or a different spouse, or job, or even analyst. Gradually we begin to realize that if we go far enough we are not the authors of our own destiny. We do not create it; we *discover* it. Likewise, human unity is not something we are called to create. We only have to recognize it when we find it.

Fairy tales, along with myths and legends, represent human problems and human development. They give us signposts to help us on our way or to guide us when we have gone astray. The following story is from Norway and illustrates a man's journey during his individuation to increasing levels of maturity symbolized by the FATHER as we have discussed him. It is a good way to summarize some of the points I have made so far.

The Seventh Father of the House[16]

There was once a man who was traveling. He came, at last, to a beautiful big farm. It had a manor house so fine that it could easily have been a small castle.

"This will be a good place to rest," he said to himself as he went in through the gate. An old man, with gray hair and beard, was chopping wood nearby.

"Good evening, father," said the traveler. "Can you put me up for the night?"

"I'm not the father of the house," said the old one. "Go into the kitchen and talk to my father."

The traveler went into the kitchen. There he found a man who was even older, down on his knees in front of the hearth, blowing on the fire.

"Good evening, father. Can you put me up for the night?" said the traveler.

"I'm not the father of the house," said the old fellow. "But go in and talk to my father. He's sitting by the table in the parlor."

So the traveler went into the parlor and talked to the man who was sitting by the table. He was much older than both the others, and he sat, shivering and shaking, his teeth chattering, reading from a big book almost like a little child.

"Good evening, father. Will you put me up for the night?" said the man.

"I'm not the father of the house, but talk to my father who's sitting on the settle," said the old man who sat by the table, shivering and shaking, his teeth chattering.

So the traveler went over to the one who was sitting on the settle, and he was busy trying to smoke a pipe of tobacco. But he was so huddled up and his hands shook so that he could hardly hold on to the pipe.

"Good evening, father," said the traveler again. "Can you put me up for the night?"

"I'm not the father of the house," replied the huddled-up old fellow. "But talk to my father who's lying in the bed."

The traveler went over to the bed, and there lay an old, old man in whom there was no sign of life but a pair of big eyes.

"Good evening, father. Can you put me up for the night?" said the traveler.

"I'm not the father of the house, but talk to my father who's lying in the cradle," said the man with the big eyes.

Well, the traveler went over to the cradle. There lay an ancient fellow, so shriveled up that he was no bigger than a baby. And there was no way of telling there was life in him except for a rattle in his throat now and then.

"Good evening, father. Can you put me up for the night?" said the man.

It took a long time before he got an answer, and even longer before the fellow finished it. He said—he like all the others—that he was not the father of the house. "But talk to my father. He's hanging in the horn on the wall."

The traveler stared up along the walls, and at last he caught sight of the horn, too. But when he tried to see the one who was lying in it, there was nothing to be seen but a little ash-white form that had the likeness of a human face.

Then he was so frightened that he cried aloud, "GOOD EVENING, FATHER! WILL YOU PUT ME UP FOR THE NIGHT?"

There was a squeaking sound up in the horn like a tiny titmouse, and it was all he could do to make out that the sound meant "Yes, my child."

Then in came a table decked with the costliest dishes, and with ale and spirits, too. And when the traveler had eaten and drunk, in came a good bed covered with reindeer hides. And he was very glad that at last he had found the true father of the house.

This lovely little tale clearly shows the importance and eternal nature of the father search. Seven, an old friend to symbologists, is related to growth, fertility, development to completion, transformation, and consciousness. Whenever seven appears in a dream, picture, or story, we can assume that some transformation is at work, some development in the direction of higher consciousness and toward individuation.

The story begins with a man, which means it is an adult who is developing. This man is clearly on a journey—if he were on a short trip he probably would have planned to stop with friends or to stay on at an inn rather than look for hospitality at a strange manor house. He is no longer home tending the farm, the business, or the family. In some manner, he has answered the call the rich young man sadly refused.

The journeyman's final sleep seems to have something of the peace of eternity. Or it may be the peace of being at home within ourselves and in life. In Christian literature there is a special quality of rest given by God to those in close harmony and fellowship with their Lord. Psychologically we could surmise that the man is longing for close harmony and fellowship with the Self. The image of the castle reinforces this view, as castles often symbolize the Self we are trying to get to or live in.

The gray hair of the old men, as well as the progression of them as FATHERS, leads us to the ancient tradition, the wisdom of fatherhood and its important part in the individuation journey. As the first old father is chopping wood, we also can imagine that the fuel for our inner nourishment must be hewn from our own nature with our own work. We cannot buy it ready-made at workshops or bookstores, even though we may find some excellent tinder there.

There are no women in this story, although they are repeatedly implied in that there must have been wives and mothers for all of these generations. Moreover, the aging and its effect on the body suggests the cycles of nature, a concept usually tied to the feminine. The farm and castle also may symbolize the feminine as nature and container, nourishing and protective. Certainly the feminine is vital to life and individuation, and an aborted masculine development deeply affects the feminine. However, this book is about our FATHER issues, and plenty of others are being written about the feminine.

In the development of this book I have presented seven general concerns of fatherhood or of the FATHER image as we try to understand and integrate it into our lives. Roughly, I would summarize these concerns as follows:

1. Protecting and supporting new life so that it can grow securely.

2. Providing a separate other to help his children differentiate from the mother and internalize their self-recognition as persons.

3. Training and preparing the young to enter and participate in life.

4. Standing for the values that give form and meaning to life.

5. Unifying the culture with impersonal justice through authority, law, and order—a collective implementation and appreciation of values. Being a Father.

6. Teaching and embodying the art of living by leavening the social forms with play, joy, spontaneity, and compassion, and combining power, wisdom, and love. Being a Grandfather or Wise Old Man.

7. Discovering and embodying the Transcendent FATHER or GREAT FATHER archetype who is the GREAT LIFE GIVER. He is the father of creativity, renewal, and regeneration (and, of course, a MOTHER is also necessary.) He combines symbolically the images of the wise old man and the CHILD as a symbol of the Self and the FATHER and the SON in the cycle of eternal sonship.

Of course, we must seek out the meaning of fatherhood in all of its forms in both our inner and outer worlds. For instance, we must not only protect and support the new life of our own infants, we also must protect the field where our own masculine and feminine principles encounter one another to produce new life in ourselves. We must provide an ambiance where this new life (often symbolized by infants and children in dreams) can grow. We must help the growing products of our own inner creativity differentiate and gain their own life and form. We must teach and initiate them, bringing them into maturity and the life we are living. Finally, we must increase our wisdom and creativity so that we can participate in the story of life.

To be worthwhile, our values must be leavened by love, compassion, and art. Otherwise the great values of the Fathers like self-discipline, which is indispensable for the development of self-knowledge, degenerate into a negative, compulsive virtues with large shadow compensations often expressed as malignant aggression.

The journeyman in this tale keeps seeking, keeps asking where the father of the house is. This reminds me of the Grail quest of Perceval and his need to continue until he asks the right question. The Grail, Joseph Campbell notes, is only attained by those who have lived their own lives. And just as both Perceval and our journeyman are rewarded with a great feast, so our inner journey will renew both our inner and outer lives. The peace of Christ no longer resides in the outer world of our ego with its fears and desires, but will be perpetually reborn in the inner world through the encounter with the images from the unconscious and the Self.

A great deal of the journey to the FATHER is individual inner work and always has been. It was, however, the task of the fathers and grandfathers to connect us to this search or journey. Now the fathers and grandfathers have left us lost and abandoned spiritually, and this is where much of our grief and confusion lies. We must not accept the easy psychological answers of symbolically killing the father, forgiving him, or reconciling with him. All of these may be necessary with the man who was our literal father, but we must go further. Nor must we make the mistake of wanting the Fathers, or worse, our institutions, to guide us to the end. If we do, we are in danger of losing the art of living.

This journey is a natural one, and if we refuse it, our psychic development will go on anyway. This development can be dreadful if we do not consciously make room for it. If we cling to shallow consciousness, the transformative power of our growth goes into our shadows, both personal and cultural, and the seeds of renewal grow instead into chaos, fragmentation, violence, and illness and the only hope we have of transforming our lives is through catastrophes (or events we perceive to be catastrophic) in our outer life.

A man who stops, as the rich young man did, at the level of the Fathers, may appear as a model of decency, responsibility, and good will, but he becomes a "desecrater of the holy of holies within." He has become fossilized in forms, and in such a case the women in his life will rebel. His inner woman will turn moody, his wife witchy, and his sons and daughters will act out or wither away. But if a man accepts his individuation and the tradition of fatherhood, if he sells all and follows Christ, he will find life eternal.

9

A Heart of Love: Reconciliation and the Spirit of Fatherhood

In our most private and most subjective lives we are not only the passive witnesses of our age, and its suffering, but also its makers.

—C. G. Jung

The poetry and art of ancient Greece rose like a fountain from the image-making creativity of human nature. It ascended at a turning point in human evolution, outlining the nature of our development in the living art of its time. While the culture of ancient Greece has passed into history, the symbolic imagery of this epoch has never failed us. It stands like a beacon that always gives hope in a storm and the inklings of a way forward if we can bring meaning to these images in our time. The Odyssean pattern, as we have seen, is in the spirit of each of us. As *The Odyssey* comes to a close, we find a series of the most compelling scenes of reconciliation in the human story.

The reconciliations lead to different levels of fourfoldedness in the dimensions of the story and ourselves. Fourfoldedness is the primal structure that has symbolized wholeness throughout time. A multitude of examples support this symbolism, but I will only mention a few. In ancient Greek philosophy, four essential elements were believed to constitute life–earth, fire, air, and water. In Egypt, the pyramids had a four-sided base. In Christianity, the cross has four points, pointing to four dimensions. In science, the four basic elements of the atmosphere are carbon, hydrogen, nitrogen, and oxygen. We orient ourselves using the four points of the compass, and we perceive in four dimensions, three in space and one in time. Fourfoldedness structures every level of our living experience.

As we approach the end of this tale, four great reconciliations take place. The first is with Odysseus and son, then with his father, then his wife Penelope, and then with the people of his kingdom. This fourfold reconciliation has great significance for it is bringing us to a symbolic reconciliation within ourselves. The unity of our nature is not a pop-psychology slogan when looked at in this perspective because fourfoldedness is a principle to which all natural processes bear witness.

As Odysseus reunites with Penelope, a wholeness of the personality is retained as the extremes of the human psyche can embrace. This embrace means to love life at a deeper and more differentiated level. This reconciliation is not simply the love of a man and wife (the level at which a modern story would end). It means, on a much more profound level, to embrace LIFE, to love life with consciousness and wholeness in a personally differentiated manner.

We then find another level of fourfoldedness—the one that is the focus of this book. Father, son, and grandfather reconcile, and kingship (Odysseus' higher self) is reclaimed. All is reconciled under the thundering approval of Zeus, who represents the great life-giving archetype. The appearance of Zeus and his approval sanctions a new era in the spirit of these reconciliations.

It may seen odd that this new era requires a final bloodbath as Odysseus kills the suitors. But we must remember the nature of sacrifice in human development. Blood sacrifices in early times were thought to be healing and to cause life's energy to come back to us at a deeper level. They were offered to the gods in an effort toward reconciliation and wholeness. They remind us that the road to wholeness and even to joy is difficult and requires a continual willingness to sacrifice. We might imagine that symbolically this was a sacrifice of those parts of our nature which detract from our unity by desiring an easy ride to kingship—a sacrifice sanctioned by Zeus, the creative principle of life.

The "longing for home" rests in the heart of all of us and it is an urgency of the heart for wholeness, for feeling at home in the world and within ourselves. This urgency fuels our personal odyssey which Jungians term the individuation process. The reconciliation of past, present, and future, mediated by wisdom and courage under the auspices of the GREAT FATHER archetype, frees us from being prisoners of our past, allows us to discover the future and live the central principles of our lives.

The journey of FATHERHOOD is to bring life into being by having it become conscious of itself. The Odyssean journey shows us how to become more conscious of ourselves through the challenges, struggles, pleasures, and pains of life. The initiating aspects of this journey bring us to an increased capacity for becoming. In the beginning, we are all "Nobody." Paradoxically, we must sacrifice the somebody that we grow to approximate in the eyes of ourselves and others in order to emerge into our true selves. The journey brings us to a point of more consciousness, more differentiation, a feeling of being more fully ourselves and a greater capacity for "I" and "thou" relationships both within and without ourselves.

These reconciliations were not the end of Odysseus' story. He went on to further reconciliations with old enemies, atonement to all the gods, great and small, and another new orientation toward life–the ability to live with a heart of love at every level of his being. But we will leave him at this point.

As fathers, we must choose between seeking out and living out our enlarged awareness or seeing it lethally diminish in our homes and communities. This awareness includes a deeper understanding of ourselves and our place in life and accepting the responsibility such knowledge brings. If we choose not to bring our knowledge and understanding into the actuality of our daily lives, we have failed a moral imperative of FATHERHOOD. In the manner we have been discussing, the path of individuation leads us more deeply into ourselves, more fully into life, and we live with a more profound sense of responsibility in the world. We become one of the Great Life Givers.

The Spirit of Fatherhood

Many of us fail at the art of living because we never realized when we were at a fork in the road. We weren't aware that every day life asks us questions beginning long before our consciousness is fully developed, and that our answers to those questions affect the foundation of our lives. We are born into a world that immediately begins to shape and form us even though it takes almost twenty years before we are mature enough to recognize the fact. During this time each of our decisions has begun to narrow our path.

Little decisions such as who we play with, why we work for grades, and what hobbies we take up, all make us collaborators in the formation and the demise of our own spirit. If we play with the "right" kids, play the "right" sports, take the "right" lessons, and later date the "right" girls or boys (or the wrong ones for the sake of rebellion), we gradually sell out our integrity and undermine our self-worth. The inner voices of integrity and conscience weaken against the so-called "mature" opinions around us, cultural pressure, and the fearful appearance of the world. Obsession with practicality, sensibleness, the promise of happiness with success, and the avoidance of pain and suffering mean we never take the byways that could add depth, meaning, and vitality to our existence. By the time we're adults, we're so embedded in our cultural direction that admitting we were wrong and beginning again will totally disrupt our lives.

In order to break this pattern we must renew our contact with the archetype of FATHER and the GREAT FATHER. Often we pause, shift our perspective and deepen our connection to LIFE because of the death of a parent or we may find the inner voice from our own center, our dreams, trying to get our attention.

Such was my own case when my dad died. I was in my early forties. Our relationship had been full of joys, sorrows, and conflicts. Many of these conflicts were never resolved and worked themselves out in a series of dreams I had after his death. The series ended with this final dream:

> *I am in the kitchen with my sister. I hear a noise in the carport. I have to kick the garbage away from the door to open it. My stepmother comes in. She says, "Buddy, he's back." I go out to meet him with tears streaming down my cheeks. I put*

my arm around his shoulder, saying, "I'm glad
you're back; there is so much I want to say to
you." He says, "There's more than one way to
die."

That final sentence, "There's more than one way to die," has
haunted me every day in every decision I have made since then.
This dream told me about the spirit of fatherhood in a way my
dad never could have in real life because he wanted me to be
secure and to suffer less than he did. Without realizing it, though,
he was protecting me from the eternal questions:

What is the purpose of my life?

Why am I here?

What am I doing?

What does my heart say?

How do I live?

Each time I avoided these questions, I discovered another
way to die—an insidious death of the spirit, even though my body
still functioned.

If we ask these questions, we force ourselves to live creatively, force ourselves to listen to our inner voices, forces
ourselves to listen to our inner integrity asking, "Is this right, or
is this wrong?" Then, when we sacrifice part of ourselves, we do
it knowingly, because we have asked the right questions. We all
have to make choices because we cannot have or do it all. But
because we've asked the right questions, we don't have to take
a poll like a modern politician to find out what we want to do. We
have our own values. We know what we want to do because we
know who we are.

The spirit of fatherhood calls us beyond the limits of the
everyday world of obligation and practicality. It doesn't deny
the value of these parts of life or claim they are easy to walk away
from. In fact, the spirit of fatherhood first calls us into them, to
become competent participants in the world of the living. We
are called upon to dream, grow, and create. We are called upon

to find the unforeseen potential that lurks within all of us, and bring it forth with strength and purpose, in a manner that substantiates ourselves and contributes to culture.

Then we are summoned to transcend this level of living and the precious self-image we have developed in it (whether we are ministers, bank presidents, or rebel poets). The questions above remain the same, but their context and our perspective on them must change as our life evolves. If we embrace this change and hold the tension between our practical and spiritual identities, our ethics and our truth, we will know the suffering that leads to wisdom. Facing the fact of death and living with the shadow of death over us inspires our lives to purpose and meaning.

This spirit of fatherhood empowers us in our experience of living with strength and purpose, grounded in personal authenticity and aware of values greater than ourselves. In turn, we empower those around us to passionate and creative living.

Notes

(Full bibliographical details appear in the **Bibliography**.)

Abbreviation: C. W. = C. G. Jung. 1959. *The Collected Works.* Translated by R. F. C. Hull, edited by H. Read, M. Fordham, G. Adler, William McGuire. Bollingen Series XX, Vols. 1– 20 (Princeton: Princeton University Press and London: Routledge and Kegan Paul), paragraph numbers.

INTRODUCTION
[1]Mircea. Eliade, *Images and Symbols,* p. 161.1

1 AN IMAGE LOST, A CHALLENGE DISCOVERED
[1]This summary is my own and I would suggest that you read the entire epic yourself. I used the version of *The Odyssey* translated by Robert Fitzgerald and relied on the article on "Odysseus" in Vol. 1, *Mythologies,* compiled by Y. Bonnefoy, pp. 494-98.
[2]Joseph Campbell, *The Hero with a Thousand Faces,* p. 51.

2 THE CHAIN OF SUFFERING AND ILLUSIONS OF HEALING

3 THE MEANING OF FATHERHOOD: A VISION OB-SCURED
[1]Daniel Levinson, *The Seasons of a Man's Life.*
[2]Joseph Campbell, *The Power of Myth,* p. 62.
[3]Mircea Eliade, *Rites and Symbols of Initiation.*
[4]Joseph Campbell, *The Power of Myth.*
[5]Evelyn Underhill, *Mysticism,* p. 147.

[6] Aleksandr Solzhenitsyn, "A World Split Apart."
[7] Helen Luke, *The Voice Within*, pp. 82, 83.
[8] Joseph Campbell, *The Hero with a Thousand Faces*, p. 11.
[9] C. G. Jung, C. W., Vol. 8, 633, 642, 645-48.
[10] C. G. Jung, C. W., Vol. 8, 645-48.
[11] Irving Yalom, *Love's Executioner and Other Tales*, p. 119.
[12] Joseph Campbell, *The Power of Myth*, p. 119.
[13] C. G. Jung, C. W., Vol. 7, 14.
[14] Mircea Eliade, *The Sacred and the Profane.*

4 PAST, PRESENT AND FUTURE: LIFE'S PERSPECTIVE

[1] Joseph Campbell, *The Hero with a Thousand Faces*, p. 388.
[2] C. G. Jung, C. W., Vol. 7, 71.
[3] Thomas Moore, ed., *A Blue Fire: Selected Writings of James Hillman*, p. 240.
[4] Aeschylus, *The Agamemnon of Aeschylus*, p. 19.
[5] Joseph Campbell, *The Hero with a Thousand Faces*, p. 353.
[6] Edward Edinger, *Ego and Archetype.*

5 MARKING THE TERRITORY: THE PSYCHOLOGY OF FATHERHOOD

[1] Joseph Campbell, *The Hero's Journey*, p. 3.
[2] D. W. Winnicott, *The Maturational Processes and the Facilitating Environment.*
[3] Homer, *The Odyssey*, p. 295.
[4] Ibid.
[5] Ibid., p. 296.
[6] C. G. Jung, C. W., Vol. 10, 65.

6 FACE TO FACE–TOE TO TOE: THE SEARCH FOR IDENTITY

[1] R. D. Laing, *Self and Others*, p. 138.
[2] Parker Palmer, *To Know As We Are Known*, p. 26.
[3] Iron Maiden, "Only the Good Die Young."
[4] Firtz Zorn, *Mars*, p. 219.
[5] Jacob Neusner, *The Bible and Us*, p. 74.
[6] Robert Bly, *Iron John*, p. 32.
[7] C. G. Jung, C. W., Vol. 9i, 43.

7 FATHERHOOD AND THE COURAGE TO STAND FOR LIFE

[1]Aleksandr Solzhenitsyn, "A World Split Apart," 1978.
[2]Ibid., p. 16.
[3]Ibid., p. 17.
[4]Eric Fromm, *The Heart of Man.*
[5]C. G. Jung, C. W., Vol. 10, 65.
[6]N. H. Kleinbaum, *Dead Poet's Society*, p. 142.
[7]Marie Louise von Franz, "Love, War and Transformation," p. 57.
[8]C. S. Hall & G. Lindzey, *Theories of Personality*, p. 114, 160.

8 A HEART OF FLAME: TRANSFORMATION AND THE TRANSCENDENT FATHER

[1]Robert Bly, *Iron John*, p. 22.
[2]Jean Bolen, *Gods in Every Man*, p. 48.
[3]M. P. O. Marford & R. J. Lenardon, *Classical Mythology*, p. 84.
[4]Walter Burkert, *Greek Religion*, p. 131.
[5]Rollo May, *The Courage to Create*, p. 98.
[6]M. P. O. Marford & R. J. Lenardon, *Classical Mythology*, p. 57.
[7]Helen Luke, *The Voice Within*, p. 41.
[8]Ibid.
[9]Joseph Campbell, *Transformation of Myth Through Time*, p. 258.
[10]Gospel of Luke 18:18.
[11]Erich Neuman, *The Origins and History of Consciousness*, p. 172.
[12]Viktor Frankl, *The Unheard Cry for Meaning*, p. 35.
[13]Joseph Campbell, *The Hero with a Thousand Faces*, p. 147.
[14]Ibid., p. 146.
[15]E. F. Schumacher, *A Guide for the Perplexed*, p. 85.
[16]J. Yolen, *Favorite Folk Tales from Around the World*, p. 59.

9 A HEART OF LOVE: RECONCILIATION AND THE SPIRIT OF FATHERHOOD

None.

Bibliography

Aeschylus, *The Agamemnon of Aeschylus.* Translated by Louis MacNeice. New York: Harcourt, Brace and Co., Faber and Faber Ltd.

Bloom, A. 1987. *The Closing of the American Mind.* New York: Simon & Schuster.

Bly, R., *Iron John: A Book About Men.* New York: Addison-Wesley.

Bolen, J.S. 1989. *Gods in Every Man.* San Francisco: Harper & Row.

Bonnefoy, Y. 1991.*Mythologies.* Compiled by Y. Bonnefoy under the direction of W. Donniger. Chicago: University of Chicago.

Burkert, W. 1985. *Greek Religion.* Translated by J. Raffan. Massachusetts: Harvard.

Campbell, J. 1973. *The Hero with a Thousand Faces.* Princeton: Bollingen Series, Princeton University Press.

Campbell, J. 1988. *Historical Atlas of World Mythology,* Vol. II, Part I. New York: Harper and Row.

Campbell, J. 1988. *The Power of Myth.* With Bill Moyers. New York: Doubleday.

Campbell, J. 1990. *The Hero's Journey.* Edited by P. Cousineau. San Francisco: Harper and Row.

Campbell, J. 1990. *Transformation of Myth Through Time.* New York: Harper and Row.

Edinger, E. F. 1972. *Ego and Archetype.* New York: Penguin.

Eliade, M. 1957. *The Sacred and the Profane.* New York: Harcourt Brace Jovanovich.

Eliade, M. 1958. *Rites and Symbols of Initiation.* New York: Harper and Row.

Eliade, M. 1991. *Images and Symbols: Studies in Religious Symbolism.* Princeton: Princeton University Press.

Erikson, E. H. 1982. *The Life Cycle Completed.* New York: W. W. Norton.

Frankl, V. E. 1975. *The Unheard Cry for Meaning: Psychotherapy and Humanism.* New York: Simon and Schuster.

von Franz, M. L. 1991. "Love, War and Transformation." *Psychological Perspectives.* Issue 24. Los Angeles: C. G. Jung Institute.

Fromm, E. 1964. *The Heart of Man.* New York: Harper and Row.

Greely, A. M. & Neusner, J. 1990. *The Bible and Us: A Priest and a Rabbi Read Scripture Together.* New York: Warner.

Hall, C. S. & Lindzey, G. 1970. *Theories of Personality.* 2nd edition. New York: John Wiley & Sons, Inc.

Harris, S. & Dickinson, B. 1988. "Only the Good Die Young," words and music. Recording, *Seventh Son of the Seventh Son:* Iron Maiden. 7902584 EMI Holland. Producer Martin Birch.

Homer. 1961. *The Odyssey.* Translated by R. Fitzgerald. New York: Doubleday, Anchor.

Jung, C. G. 1959. *The Collected Works.* Translated by R. F. C. Hull, edited by H. Read, M. Fordham, G. Adler, William McGuire. Bollingen Series XX, Vols. 1–20. Princeton: Princeton University Press. London: Routledge and Kegan Paul.

Jung, C.G. (conceived and ed.). 1964. *Man and His Symbols.* New York: Doubleday.

Jung, C.G. 1973. *Memories, Dreams, Reflections.* Recorded and edited by Aniela Jaffe, translated by R. Winston & C. Winston. New York: Pantheon-Random House.

Kleinbaum, N. H. 1989. *Dead Poet's Society.* New York: Bantam.

Laing, R. D. 1971. *Self and Others.* 2nd ed. Harmondsworth, England: Penguin.

Levinson, D. J. 1978. *The Seasons of a Man's Life.* New York: Ballantine.

Luke, H. M. 1988. *The Voice Within.* New York: Crossroad.

May, R. 1975. *The Courage to Create.* New York: Norton.

Marford, M. P. O. & Lenardon, R. J. 1945. *Classical Mythology.* 3rd ed. New York: Longman.

Moore, R. & Gillette, D. 1990. *King, Warrior, Magician, Lover.* San Francisco: Harper.

Moore, T. (ed.) 1989. *A Blue Fire: Selected Writings of James Hillman.* New York: Harper Perennial.

Neumann, E. 1973. *The Origins and History of Consciousness.* Princeton: Bollingen Series, Princeton University Press.

Palmer, P. J. 1983. *To Know As We Are Known: A Spirituality of Education.* San Francisco: Harper.

Schumacher, E. F. 1977. *A Guide for the Perplexed.* New York: Harper & Row.

Solzhenitsyn, A. 1978, June 8. *A World Split Apart.* Commencement Address at Harvard University (New York: Harper & Row).

Underhill, E. 1914. *Practical Mysticism.* Columbus, Ohio: Ariel Press.

Underhill, E. 1955. *Mysticism.* New York: Penguin.

Winnicott, D. W. 1965. *The Maturational Processes and the Facilitating Environment.* New York: International Universities Press.

Yalom, I. D. 1989. *Love's Executioner and Other Tales of Psychotherapy.* New York: Basic Books.

Yolen, J., ed. 1986. *Favorite Folk Tales from Around the World.* New York: Pantheon.

Zorn, F. 1982. *Mars.* New York: Alfred A. Knopf.

Index

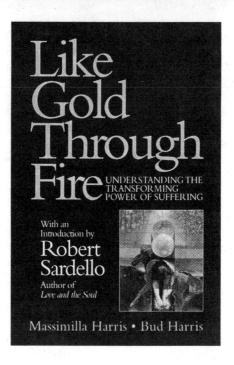

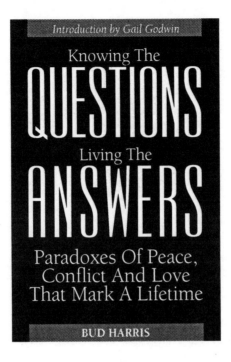